A BRIEF HISTORY OF THE CZECH LANDS TO 2000

PETR ČORNEJ

JIŘÍ POKORNÝ

PRÁH

ISBN 80-7252-026-1

Historically, the Czech Republic (78,864 km² in surface area) is made up of three parts: Bohemia, Moravia, and part of Silesia, which together are known as the Czech Lands. These lands became part of a single state, or more precisely joint state, in the Middle Ages, and remained so for centuries. The territory of what today is the Slovak Republic, however, was from roughly 1000 AD to the Autumn of 1918 an integral part of the Kingdom of Hungary, and its position changed radically only with the establishment of the Czechoslovak Republic in the Autumn of 1918. The history of the Czech Lands and Slovakia does not, therefore, make up an organic whole and it would be misleading and indeed impossible to try to produce a unified account of the development of both countries. This means that the following account will concentrate systematically on the historical development of Bohemia, Moravia and Silesia, and consider Slovakia only after the birth of Czechoslovakia, mentioning earlier Slovak history only when relevant.

The Czech Lands

Geographically, the territories of Bohemia on the one hand and Moravia with part of Silesia on the other, differ quite markedly. Bohemia is enclosed by mountain ranges, remnants of the Palaeozoic mountains (the Šumava, the Krušné Mountains, the Lužic Mountains, the Jizerské Mountains, the Broumov Mountains, the Czecho-Moravian Uplands), while Moravia (if we leave aside Jeseníky) consists principally of lowlands opening into the Austrian Lands and the Slovak Danubian basin. Bohemia was already settled in the earlier Stone Age (the earliest human remains on Bohemian territory are more than 17,000 years old) but archaeological finds here are eclipsed by the more dramatic evidence of ancient "mammoth hunters" in Moravia, especially in Předmostí by Přerov, Pavlov and Dolní Věstonice from a period more than 26,000–22,000 years ago. Naturally, the sources increase as the present comes closer. In the period of the rise of Ancient Rome (3rd – 1st Century

The Czech Lands in prehistoric times

Celts and German Tribes

BC), Czech territory was conquered by the Celtic tribe of the Boii, and it was from this that the Latin name "Bohemia" (and later the German name Böhmen) is derived. In the first years of the 1st Millennium AD, a time of increasing pressure from the Roman Empire, the Celts were replaced by the German tribe known as Marcomans, whose ruler Marobud fought with the Romans (17 AD). Bohemia and Moravia remained, however, outside the Roman Empire, and the latter's fortified borders (the limes Romanus), only touched the edge of the territory at Mušov in South Moravia). The Czech Lands did not therefore come into any

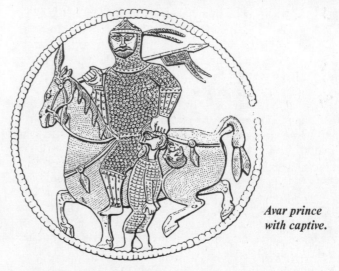

Avar prince with captive.

systematic contact with the Ancient World, and this was reflected in their later cultural development.

Turn of the 5th-6th Century
Arrival of the Slavs

■ The ensuing centuries of what are known as the Great Migrations fundamentally changed the ethnic composition of the population of Bohemia and Moravia. In the 6th century Slav tribes, displaced from the south-west by the German Langobard and Thuringian tribes, began to penetrate into the Slovak and Moravian lowlands and the Bohemian basin. Archaeological finds from this period are scarce. One of the few pieces of evidence that survive is a reference to the presence of Slav tribes in the Czech Lands around 512 in the work of the Byzantine historian Procopius, but the report cannot be verified. In some regions the Slavs and Germans lived side by side for a certain period, but this coexistence was interrupted from the beginning by the incursions of the Avars – Turko-Tartar nomads who seized Panonia (the Latin geographical term for the part of today's Hungary that is west of the Danube), and undertook raids into the Frankish Empire. All these changes speeded up the disapearance of German ethnic groups on Czecho-Moravian territory. Members of the German tribes either left or merged with the Slavs, who became the sole population of the area.

■ The different way of life characteristic of the Slav tribes and the neighbouring Avars necessarily led to mutual conflicts. While the Slavs lived in agricultural settlements, the nomadic Avars were more mobile and more belligerent, and even subjugated part of the Slav population. Sometime around 620 the Slav tribes rose in rebellion against Avar rule.

■ The rebels were strikingly successful in 623-624, when they found a leader in the form of the Frankish Prince Samo, who probably came from what today is Central France. After the Avars had been repulsed, the united Slav tribes acknowledged Samo as ruler and head of a large empire that included the territories of Boehmia, Moravia, part of Slovakia and apparently even a part of Bavaria settled at that time by Slavs. It was the first empire to be created by the western Slavs, but it was probably less a state in the true sense of the word than a tribal alliance, united by the person of the ruler. Its centre seems to have been situated in the South Moravian lowlands around the River Morava, where fortified settlements had already emerged. Samo ruled for nearly twenty-five years and led a successful defensive war against Dagobert, King of the Franks, whose forces he defeated in 631 near the stronghold of Vogastiburg (possibly in North-West Bohemia). After Samo's death, which occurred sometime in 658-659, his empire disintegrated.

■ For the next 150 years there is a dearth of written reports of the Czech Lands. Only from the 830s do the sources speak more clearly. At this time the core of the political entity historians have called the Greater Moravian Empire emerged around the lower reaches of the Morava River. The epithet was the artificial creation of later times, however, and contemporary authors speak only of Moravia and Moravians.

■ The first known Greater Moravian ruler was Mojmír I, who after 833 annexed the Nitran reagion in South Slovakia to his territory. At this time Christian missions, mainly sent from Bavaria and the Salzburg region, were already active in Mojmír's empire. It was chiefly the princes with their families and armed retainers who accepted the new religion, while most of the ordinary people continued to worship the pagan gods. Greater Moravia reached its territorial apogee under Mojmír's successors, who in addition

623-624
Empire of Samo

830-836
Birth of the
Greater Moravian
Empire

Cyril and Methodius (on the left), in front of Christ.
Fresco from the 11th Century in San Clemente in Rome.

to maintaining the original centre and South Slovakia, brought the Slav tribes in Bohemia, Panonia and the area around the River Vistula in what is now Poland under Moravian sovereignty. The centres of political, cultural and religious life were the South Moravian strongholds, Mikulčice and Staré Město (near today's Uherské Hradiště).

**863
Mission of Cyril
and Methodius**

■   Mojmír's successor Rostislav tried to create a counterweight to the influence of the East Frankish Empire in Central Europe, and he therefore systematically cultivated relations with Byzantium. This included a request for a Christian mission from the Byzantine Empire, which arrived under the leadership of the brothers Constantine (who later took the name Cyril as his monastic name) and Methodius, originally Greeks from Thessalonike. They came to Moravia in 863 and began to propagate a Slav liturgy comprehensible to all the population. For this purpose Constantine put together an artificial Slavonic language (known as Old Slavonic or Church Slavonic) on the basis of the South Slav dialect, and created a special script for it (Glagolitic). Together with his brother he then translated liturgical texts and the New Testament into Old Slavonic, and it is not impossible that he translated the entire Bible, although direct evidence is lacking. Later Methodius was appointed Archbishop of the Moravian-Panonian Archdiocese. His seat was a church at Velehrad (apparently at what is now Sada by Uherské Hradiště, where archaeologists have uncovered the foundations of a large sanctuary). Both the brothers from Thessalonike were later canonised.

■ After the death of Methodius (6. 4. 885), Prince Svatopluk, who succeeded Rostislav, repudiated the supporters of the Slavonic liturgy and once again endorsed the Latin rite. Not long before his death, Methodius had managed to baptise the Czech princeling Bořivoj and his wife Ludmila, and the Slavonic liturgy did not die with him. His pupils worked in Bohemia and other Slav areas, and the Slavonic liturgy later put down roots in Kievan Rus. Its progress was aided by the creation of a new script, known as Cyrillic, the precursor of the modern Cyrillic alphabet.

885
Death of Methodius

■ Svatopluk died in 894 and was succeeded by his son Mojmír II, but conditions became much worse, since the turn of the 9th/10th Century was the period at which the nomadic Magyars (Huns) attacked Central Europe. Several of the tribal princes exploited the external threat to Moravia to free themselves from Moravian overlords hip. In 895, soon after Svatopluk's death, the Czech princes, including Bořivoj's son Spytihněv, took an oath of vassalage to Arnulf, King of the Eastern Franks. After years of fighting, the Greater Moravian Empire succumbed to the Hungarian raiders around 907. The Hungarians, however, did not settle the core of Moravian territory but retreated to the extensive

907
Fall of Greater Moravia

Hypothetical reconstruction of the stronghold in Mikulčice, probably the centre of Greater Moravia.

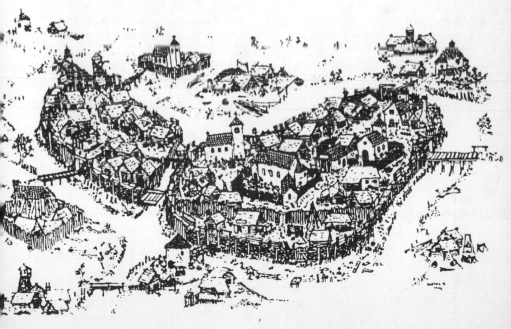

West Slavonic warriors of the 10th – 11th centuries.

lowlands around the Rivers Tisa and Danube. In Europe, this was the final episode in the period of the Great Migrations. Greater Moravia left behind a remarkable cultural legacy that the world has come to know only since 1945 as a result of archaeological finds. The Great Moravian Empire was not, as has sometimes been claimed, the first common state of the Czech and Slovak people, but a more or less voluntary union of Slav tribes who spoke related dialects. The process of the formation of nations and nation states in Central Europe only started after it had fallen.

End of the 9th Century
Beginnings of the Czech State

■   The newly emergent Czech state took over many Greater Moravian cultural impulses. The current debate on whether there was one Slav tribe or several living on Bohemian territory in the 9th Century is not important. In keeping with the Roman tradition, European men of learning used the general name *Bohemi* for all the inhabitants of Bohemia. The Slavonic name *Češi, Čechové (Czechs, Czechia)* appeared perhaps as late as the end of the 9th Century, and at first evidently defined the group of people who surrounded the ruling prince and shared in political power. Gradually the name was extended to apply to the whole Slav ethnic group settled in Bohemia, speaking in Czech, and forming the medieval Czech nation.

Around 885
Prague - Seat of the Czech Princes

■   The prince who presided over the birth of the Czech state was the Bořivoj already mentioned. He is the first historically documented member of the Přemyslid dynasty, which claimed to originate from the legendary prince Přemysl, supposedly a ploughman, who married the seer Libuše. Bořivoj's seat was originally at Levý Hradec (north of Prague), and it was here that after accepting baptism from the hands of Methodius he founded the Church of St. Clement, evidently the oldest in Bohemia.

Probably around the year 885 he moved his seat to a stronghold called Praha (on the site of Prague castle today). His motives were probably pragmatic, since the Prague stronghold guarded an important ford across the Vltava and it had therefore become an important trading centre. Prague has been the main political and cultural centre of the Czech state ever since.

■ Despite his key position in the Bohemian basin, Bořivoj remained to his death a loyal ally of the Greater Moravian Empire, and it was his son Spytihněv who managed to emancipate himself from Moravian overlordship. Spytihněv looked to Bavaria for support, and this policy was essentially decisive for the future orientation of Bohemia to the culture of the "Latin" west. The results of this step were not immediately apparent, however, and through the 10th and 11th Centuries two cultures – the Latin and the gradually retreating Old Slavonic – existed side by side in the Czech Lands. Spytihněv was succeeded by his brother Vratislav I, founder of the Church of St. George at Prague Castle. When he too died, disputes broke out in the ruling line. They culminated in the murder of Princess Ludmila, the widow of Bořivoj, a dreadful deed carried out on the 15th of September 921 at the stronghold of Tetín (above the River Berounka, not far from the later Karštejn Castle) by Viking warriors in the service of the princess Drahomír, widow of Vratislav I. The murdered Ludmila was later canonised and venerated especially in the Prague Basilica of St. George, where the princess's remains found a last resting place.

15th September 921
Murder of Princess
Ludmila

Prague Castle in the time of Prince Wenceslas.

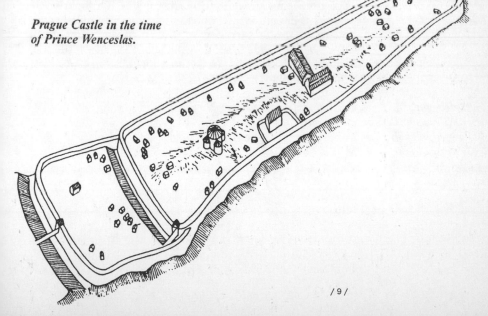

**28th September 929
Killing of Prince
Wenceslas**

■ The murder did not, however, end rivalry and violence within the Přemyslid dynasty, although at first the reign of Prince Wenceslas, son of Vratislav I and Drahomír, developed successfully. Wenceslas, an unusually educated ruler for his time, continued the expansive policy of the predecessors, changing the political line only in the sense of switching his orientation from Bavaria to Saxony, which was taking the leading role in the German territories. One expression of this tie was the founding of the Church of St. Vitus at the Prague Castle, later to be rebuilt as a Gothic cathedral. For reasons that are obscure, however, Wenceslas found himself in dispute with his younger brother Boleslav. On the 28th of September 935 (some sources state 929), Boleslav had his elder brother murdered at the stronghold of Boleslav (today Stará Boleslav), and seized the throne himself. Like his grandmother Ludmila, Wenceslas was canonised and later became the symbol of Czech statehood and its survival, the ideal and eternal ruler of Bohemia and its heavenly patron. The cult of St. Wenceslas played a major part in the development of the Czech state in the modern age and continues to be important today.

**973
Establishment
of the Bishopric
of Prague**

■ In the first phase of its existence, the Czech state reached its greatest territorial extent in the reign of Boleslav II in the late 10th century. At this point it included both Bohemia itself, Moravia and more distant areas of what are now Slovakia and Galicia. Sometime before 970 Boleslav's sister Mlada founded the first convent in the Czech Lands, for Benedictine nuns, which was built beside the Church of St. George. A little later, in 973, a bishopric was set up in Prague, which in terms of church administration meant that the territory of Bohemia was freed from dependence on the diocese of Ratisbon. The new bishopric, to which Sas Thietmar was appointed in 976, was subordinated to the Archdiocese of Mainz.

*The Rotunda
of St. Vitus at Prague
Castle, probably
destroyed in the
11th–12th century.*

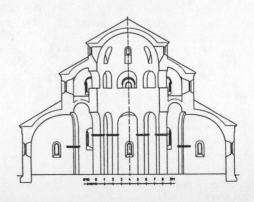

oleʒlAw) canoṛcos oꝼꝼenbṛc ꝫ omẽm oleṛũ ꝫ cṛiſhꝰanos

At this period it was usual for the secular ruler to feel superior to the highest representative of the church in his territory, and regard the latter as his chaplain. Attempts to emancipate the church were still in their infancy. In the Czech Lands it was the second Bishop of Prague, Vojtěch (Adalbert), who made great efforts to strengthen the prestige of the church and deepen understanding of the principles of Christian life (barbarian customs still survived even at the prince's court, which had accepted Christianity only superficially). Vojtěch, a highly educated and well-travelled man, was responsible for the founding of the first monastery in the territory (in 993 in Břevnov near Prague; today part of Prague district 6), where he brought members of the Benedictine order. His activities, however, met with hostility from Boleslav II, whose dislike was heightened by the fact that the bishop came from the princely line of the Slavníks, who controlled areas south and east of Prague. In 995 Boleslav's armed retainers raided the Slavník's stronghold in Libice above Cidlina and killed all the members of the family they found there, thus securing Přemyslid control of all Bohemia. Vojtěch was abroad at the time, and on the 23rd of April 997 he died a martyr's death on a missionary journey to the Baltic Prussians. On the initiative of the Emperor Otto III and the Polish King Boleslav the Brave, an archbishopric was founded at Vojtěch's tomb in Gniezno in Poland. Vojtěch, who had failed to find support in Bohemia during his lifetime, was at least acknowledged after his death. He was canonised and ranked with St. Ludmila and St. Wenceslas, whose cult he himself had propagated. Later another saint was added to this trio in the form of Abbot

Boleslav I attacking the Prince.

23rd April 997
Martyrdom of
Bishop Vojtěch

The Bishop St. Vojtěch before the Emperor Otto III.

Procop, founder of the Sazava Monastery (after 1030), the only Czech monastery using the Slavonic liturgy which survived within its walls until 1097. Prokop was not canonised until 1204, but then, together with Wenceslas, Ludmila and Vojtěch, he became part of the foursome of Czech patron saints who are venerated to this day.

**1002
Bohemia first
granted as an
Imperial Fiefdom**

■ At the turn of the 10th/11th Century the Czech state found itself in deep crisis. There were two principal reasons: above all, the rise and expansion of the new neighbouring states, Hungary and Poland, and also quarrels between the sons of Boleslav II. In the turmoil, the Přemyslids lost most of their territorial gains and their state was cut back to Bohemia itself. Boleslav the Brave of Poland exploited the weakness of the Přemyslids and in 1002 managed to install his own candidate, Vladivoj, on the throne of Prague. Vladivoj was the first Czech ruler to have his position confirmed by the Roman Emperor Henry II. He granted Vladivoj Bohemia as a Roman fief, starting a tradition maintained for many centuries.

■ The fact that the Holy Roman Emperors, who usually came of German lines, were granting Czech rulers the Czech state as a fiefdom, in no way meant the subordination of the Czech Lands and their population to Germans. The Roman Empire, revived in 967 by the Emperor Otto II, had developed from the ideals of medieval universalism and was supposed to include the whole of

Christendom, subject to the Pope spiritually and in secular terms to the power of the emperor. In practice, however, the Roman Empire (known as the Holy Roman Empire from the 12th century), was limited to what today is Austria, Switzerland, Benelux, Silesia, Bohemia, Moravia, Germany and Northern Italy, and even in these areas the political authority of the emperor, who used to receive the title after coronation in Rome, was more formal than real. The individual princes, including the ruler of the Bohemian state, remained sovereigns on their own territory. Relations between the Czech rulers and the kings or emperors of the Roman Empire were not, of course, unproblematic. In practice the amount of independence a Czech ruler enjoyed would depend on the personality and capabilities of each Czech ruler. An energetic Roman emperor usually tried to intervene in Bohemian politics, while a weak emperor would leave the Přemyslids freedom and space. Points of conflict, however, were more than frequent and often resulted in direct military confrontations.

■ This was the case in the reign of Prince Břetislav I (1034–1055), known as the Czech Achilles. He not only kidnapped his future wife Guta (Jitka in Czech) from a convent, but together with his father Oldřich reannexed Moravia to the Bohemian lands, carried out a campaign of plunder in Poland and contributed to the issue of the first Czech law book. In 1054/1055 he stipulated that the ruler in Bohemia should always be the eldest member of the Přemyslid dynasty. This was known as the principle of seniority and was later to lead to frequent disputes within the Přemyslid line. His younger sons obtained princely domains in Moravia (Brno, Olomouc and Znojmo had been developing as seats of local princelings), which contributed to the rise of historic centres that are still key today.

1054/1055
Prince Břetislav I and the Seniority Rule

■ The most famous of the sons of Břetislav I was undoubtedly Vratislav II (1061–1092). At the very start of his reign he showed his political foresight when in 1063, in an attempt to weaken the power of the Bishop of Prague, he established the bishopric of Olomouc in Moravia. In 1085, in return for his support for the Emperor Henry IV in his quarrel with Pope Gregory VII, he obtained the title of king, athough only for himself. The coronation of Vratislav was apparently the occasion for the creation of the precious illuminated mansucript known as the Vyšehrad Codex, an exquisite example of Romanesque book painting. The award of the royal title to the Czech ruler confirmed the importance of the Bohemian state in the Roman Empire and the leading position of its ruler among the feudal lords of

1085
Vratislav II, the first Czech King

that supranational political entity. Vratislav II liked to stay in Vyšehrad, the second Prague castle which had been founded on the right bank of the Vltava in the later 10th Century.

■ Among Vratislav II's successors, one of the most important was Prince Soběslav I (1125-1140) whose name is linked to the reconstruction of Prague castle as a stone Romanesque fortress. This work continued into the reign of his successor Vladislav II (1140-1172). The building affected not just Prague Castle but the face of the merchant and craftsmen's settlements below the castle, where stone houses were built and the banks of the Vltava were linked by a stone bridge named the Judith bridge – the second oldest in Central Europe. It served its purpose until it collapsed in 1342. The Romanesque architectural style was also used in the construction of monastic buildings for various religious orders (the 12th century saw the arrival in Bohemia of the Premonstratensians, whose centre became the famous Strahov Monastery near Prague Castle, the Cistercians and the Johannites.) Numerous Romanesque churches were built in other important places (e.g. the Rotunda of St. Catherine in Znojmo with its wall paintings of members of the Přemyslid dynasty) and in the Bohemian and Moravian countryside.

1158
Vladislav II,
the second Czech
King

■ Vladislav II made a greater name for himself in Europe than many other Czech rulers. As an ally of the Roman Emperor Frederick I Barbarossa he took part in the military expedition to Italy and was rewarded with a royal crown in 1158, although once again this was a purely personal grant. During his reign the process by which the Czech Lands drew culturally closer to the European West was notably strengthened.

1182
Establishment of
the Margravate of
Moravia

■ Vladislav's successors failed to develop sufficiently adroit policies towards Frederick Barbarossa, and the latter exploited their weakness to make direct interventions in Czech affairs. He viewed the Czech Lands from the point of view of the universalistic imperial ideal and behaved accordingly. In the course of the 1180s he tried to divide them into three independent units, all directly subordinate to the Roman Emperor, and turned the bishoprics of Prague (1187) and Moravia (1182) into imperial principalities, independent of the Czech ruler. This step had no serious consequences for the integraty of the Czech Lands, however, since Frederick Barbarossa soon died and his successors lacked authority. Only Moravia maintained the title of margravate granted by Frederick. From the constitutional point of view, this gave it an independent status that it

The Holy Trinity, Přemysl Otakar II, Wenceslas II,
and Wenceslas III

maintained up to the modern age, but except for one short
episode much later, in practice it always remained part of
a common state with Bohemia. The strong linkage between
the two lands was confirmed by the appointments made to
the office of Moravian margrave. Fron the very beginning
the honour was held by a member of the ruling dynasty in
Bohemia, and from 1411 almost always by the Bohemian
ruler himself.

■ Several factors contributed to making the end of the
12th Century a period of stabilisation. The most important
was the confirmation of the rights of the nobility (in what is
known as the Statutes of Prince Conrad Otto of 1189), which
was emerging as a class of free and hereditary landowners.
There was also a general economic upswing and a weakening
in the position of the Roman emperors, who now required
help from the Czech rulers rather than vice versa. This
situation was exploited by the Czech ruler Přemysl I Otakar,
who in 1198 obtained the royal title and later, in 1212,
secured the grant of a charter called the Golden Bull of
Sicily from the Holy Roman Emperor and King of Sicily. The

1212
The Golden Bull
of Sicily

text defined the relationship of the Czech state to the Holy Roman Empire, definitively granting the Czech ruler the title of monarch, and making Bohemia a kingdom rather than just a principality and also the leading state entity in the Holy Roman Empire. Already, more than a half a century before, the Czech ruler had been granted the honorary title of Imperial Arch Cup-Bearer. More important, of course, was the status of imperial elector acquired in the mid 13th Century, which made the Czech king one of the seven electors of the Holy Roman Emperor. The Czech state had set out on the road to great power status in Central Europe.

■   Such a position, however, could not have been feasible without a prosperous economy. As early as the 12th century, the systematic colonisation of previously unpopulated areas and the transformation of extensive forests and marshes into agriculturally usable land had begun, stimulated by the needs and on the initiative of the ruler, the monasteries and the nobility. This process was given a powerful new impulse in the 13th Century, when a substantial stream of colonists from overpopulated German areas started to arrive in Bohemia and Moravia (and also Silesia and the Kingdom of Hungary). The German colonists took a particularly major part in the settlement of thickly forested and relatively inaccessible borderlands. At they same time they brought more advanced agricultural techniques. Human settlements, once concentrated in the fertile lowlands, now covered the whole of Bohemia and Moravia with the exception of the high border ranges, which were not colonised until the 16th–18th Century. Colonists from the German areas also relied on a more advanced legal system which precisely defined the relations between serf farmers and feudal lords. The serfs would pay the lord fixed monetary sums on a regular twice yearly basis.

■   One aspect of colonisation was the development of a relatively dense network of royal towns (i.e. towns under the direct sovereignty of the crown) and serf towns (subject to noble or church lordship). The legal institutions of the town were also brought by the German colonists. Towns as centres of crafts and trade either emerged from settlements by important castles (in Bohemia e.g. Litoměřice and Hradec Králové; in Moravia e.g. Brno, Olomouc, Znojmo) or were established from scratch (České Budějovice, Nymburk etc.) The royal towns (by 1300 there were 32 in Bohemia and 18 in Moravia) were larger and more important. They were granted significant privileges by the ruler (the right to build fortifications, the right to markets, the right to brew beer), but their taxes were a direct source

13th Century German Colonisation

Development of the towns

of income for the royal treasury. It was in the 13th Century that the Prague agglomeration finally became formally a town, or in fact group of towns (today's Prague Old Town after 1230, The Lesser Side in 1257). The mining towns concerned with the mining and casting of precious metals, which in the Czech Lands meant principally silver, enjoyed a special position. Moravia boasted such a centre in Jihlava, but the most important deposits were at Kutná hora in Central Bohemia. The abundance of silver ore enabled the Czech ruler, with help from Italian experts, to carry out a reform of the coinage, and in 1300 to start the minting of the valuable coins known as Bohemian or Prague groschen. These replaced the older coinage minted in Bohemia since the later 10th Century.

1300
Wenceslas II
and currency
reform

■ Colonisation also caused profound change in the ethnic structure of the population in the Czech Lands. The originally compact, Czech-speaking ethnic group ceased to be the only inhabitants of Bohemian-Moravian territory. The share of the German element rose markedly and the Kingdom of Bohemia and Moravian Margravate became a common state inhabited by two peoples. This situation continued up to 1946. For seven centuries the relations between the two peoples fluctuated on a wide scale from peaceful coexistence to the mutual rivalry and competition that contributed on both sides to a sharpening of national consciousness and sometimes even to expressions of nationalism chauvinism and xenophobia.

Changes in
ethnic structure

■ In the course of the 13th Century the Czech Lands also accepted the more advanced culture of Western Europe, characterised by the Gothic style. The ruler and nobility adopted the courtly-chivalric way of life and started to build stone castles (e.g. Bezděz, Zvíkov, Český Krumlov, Landštejn). Remarkable religious buildings were also constructed (the monasteries of Zlatá koruna, Vyšší Brod). One expression of deepening religious feeling was the activity of the new orders of Franciscans and Poor Clares (the monastic complex in Prague at na Františku). Přemysl I Otakar's daughter, the pious Agnes of Bohemia (died 1282), who founded the Order of the Crusaders with the Red Star, was a moving force in this direction. She was venerated in the Middle Ages, but in fact had to wait until the stirring Autumn of 1989 for canonisation. Another much reverenced woman was the noble Zdislava (died 1252), protector and healer of the poor and founder of the Dominican monasteries in Turnov and Jabloň.

Beginnings
of Gothicculture

■ The rapid rise of the Czech state was also reflected in international relations. By a combination of marriage

26th August 1278
Battle of the Moravian Field and Death of Přemysl II Otakar

policies and military pressure the Bohemian kings managed to bring the Austrian Lands under their rule, but this was not the limit of their ambitions. Přemysl II Otakar (1253–1278), whose wealth and military power earned him the nickname "king of iron and gold", also gained control of Carinthia, Styria and Carniola, and set his sights on the crown of the King of the Romans. The other electors, however, were alarmed by his increasingly strong position, and so in 1273 the prestigious title was conferred instead on Count Rudolf von Habsburg, whose line was only just beginning to come to the forefront of European politics. When Přemysl was forced to give up the Austrian and Alpine lands, military confrontation with the new imperial ruler was inevitable. On the 26th of August 1278 Přemysl II Otakar perished at the Battle of the Moravian Field.

4th August 1306
Extinction of the Přemyslids in the male line

■   The defeat slowed down the political expansion of the Bohemian state, but could not halt it. King Wenceslas II, Přemysl's son, turned his attention to the east and north. In 1300 he acquired the crown of Poland, and when the ruling Arpad dynasty in the Hungarian Lands became extinct, he managed to get his son Wenceslas crowned as King of Hungary. In 1305, however, the intelligent if illiterate Wenceslas II died, unaware that his political achievements would soon be in ruins. His only son Wenceslas II had to renounce the Hungarian crown and concentrate on maintaining his rule in Poland, where a strong opposition had emerged. During a military campaign he was murdered in Olomouc on the 4th of August 1308 in circumstances which remain obscure. His death meant the extinction of the male line of the Přemyslid dynasty, which had ruled in the Bohemian state for more than 400 years.

1310
The Luxemburgs on the Czech Throne

■   A vacant throne almost always brings danger of destabilisation, and this was precisely what happened in the Kingdom of Bohemia. Fortunately the period of turmoil was short, and in 1310 John of Luxemburg, husband of the last Přemyslid's sister, Eliška Přemysl, emerged victorious in the struggle for the throne. John was the son of the King of the Romans and later Emperor, Henry VII of Luxemburg, who died in 1313 without having been able to offer his first-born son effective assistance. The young John, who had been brought up at the French court, never got used to the Kingdom of Bohemia, and the need to stand up to the political aspirations of the self-confident Czech nobility did not increase his enthusiasm for the place. He therefore took little interest in internal politics and devoted himself to foreign policy, in which he achieved brilliant results (the

Charles IV as King of Bohemia and Margrave of Moravia

acquisition of Upper Lusatia and Silesia, and the annexation of the Cheb region).

■　　　From 1332 John's eldest son, who was originally christened Wenceslas but took the name Charles after confirmation in France, began to make a substantial political impact at his father's side. The intelligent boy had also grown up at the court in Paris, where he had been given an above-average education. In his youth he also stayed in Luxemburg and Northern Italy, and so when he returned to Bohemia in 1333 he already spoke French, Italian, German and Latin, and soon mastered Czech as well. From his arrival he systematically devoted himself to internal affairs, and his father made him co-regent. His achievements at that period included the successful campaign to have the Prague bishopric promoted to an archbishopric (in 1344), and the related reconstruction of the Church of St. Vitus at Prague Castle as a huge Gothic cathedral. At the same time Charles secured the setting up of a new bishopric with its seat in Litomyšl in East Bohemia. While his father was still alive, the Bohemian prince also took a strong part in international politics and in 1346, with the support of the Pope, he was crowned King of the Romans as Charles IV. Shortly afterwards (26th of August 1346), John of Luxemburg fell fighting for the French King against the English at the Battle of Crecy. The throne of Bohemia naturally devolved on Charles.

■　　　Charles IV (1346–1378) was the first ruler of Bohemia to become King of the Romans and, after his coronation in Rome in 1355, Holy Roman Emperor. As Roman

1344
Bishopric of Prague raised to Archbishopric

1346
Charles of Luxemburg becomes King of the Romans

King and Emperor he was theoretically the secular head of the whole of Western Christendom, and the link between this office and the Bohemian crown determined the character of his policy. From the beginning he regarded the Kingdom of Bohemia as his central power base. He made his imperial seat in this rich and consolidated country and also took excellent care of it without neglecting his obligations to other areas.

1348
Legal codification of the Bohemian Crown Lands

■ The year 1348 was an important milestone in strengthening the prestige of the Bohemian state, since Charles issued a constitutional charter that legally confirmed the creation of the Lands of the Bohemian Crown, a joint state including the Kingdom of Bohemia and what were known as the adjacent lands (Moravia, the Principality of Silesia, Upper Lusatia and from 1368 Lower Lusatia as well). This political entity, which acquired a symbol in the new and superbly adorned royal diadem (known as the St. Wenceslas crown in honour of the land's patron saint), existed in the same territorial form until 1635. Charles clearly set out the relationship of the Kingdom of Bohemia to the Holy Roman Empire in the Golden Bull for the Empire, accepted in 1355–1356. It stipulated that the ruler of Bohemia held first place among the electors. Some of the articles of Charles's Golden Bull remained in force until the final end of the Holy Roman Empire in 1806.

Spring 1348
Founding of Prague University and the Prague New Town

■ Charles chose Prague for his residence, and it therefore became the most important city of the empire and needed to be correspondingly grand. In 1348 Charles enlarged the city by building the Prague New Town on a lavish scale, and immediately founded a university in Prague, the first in Central Europe. Numerous exquisite Gothic buildings were constructed to adorn the capital. Apart from the reconstruction of the royal palace at Prague Castle and the overall reconstruction of Vyšehrad these included many churches and the magnificent Stone Bridge (now Charles Bridge), built on the site of the old Judith Bridge. On the right bank it was guarded by the remarkable Old Town Bridge Tower, the work of the architect Petr Parléř who also played a decisive role in shaping the Cathedral of St. Vitus. Roughly 30 kilometres from Prague Charles IV founded the Castle of Karlštejn as a fortress to protect the imperial crown jewels. Numerous artists contributed to the decoration of the castle, among them Master Theodoric, author of a set of 130 paintings on wood. Gothic art naturally had a major impact on many other Bohemian and Moravian towns. When Charles IV died on the 29th of November 1378, the Bohemian state was among the most powerful in Europe and had fully overcome its earlier backwardness in comparison to the western and southern European areas.

■ Shortly afterwards, however, there were reverses. In 1380 the Kingdom of Bohemia was hit by a major epidemic of Black Death, a plague which had raged in 1347–1352 in most of Europe. The once flourishing country found itself in deep crisis caused by the steep drop in population (10–15%) and its attendant economic effects (the impoverishment of the nobility, the abandonment and depopulation of whole areas). In this unexpected crisis, the state lacked an outstanding ruler, since Charles's eldest son, the educated Wenceslas IB (1378–1419), preferred pleasure to politics. The internal position of the Kingdom of Bohemia was also weakened by the monarch's disputes with representatives of the rich church and the noble magnates. The situation was exploited by some of the imperial princes, who in 1400 deposed Wenceslas from the Roman throne.

1380 Great Plague Epidemic in Bohemia

■ Bohemian society, whose cultural level had risen substantially under Charles IV, sought for the causes of this steep decline and also for a way out of the depressing conditions. Contemporary opinions and solutions were characteristic of the age, and reflective people saw the manifestations of crisis as signs of God's wrath and punishment for the violation of the principles of God's law, contained in the Bible. According to this view, the main culprit was the Church, which had been corrupted by wealth and pride, intervening in secular politics and abandoning its original pastoral mission (care for the salvation of Christian souls) and the apostolic example. The papal schism of the time seemed to justify these critical voices. The attitude of the reformist thinkers can be summarised in one sentence: if the church returns to the ideals of the New Testament, there will soon be improvement in the whole state of Bohemian society.

Crisis of the Czech state and society

■ A group of Bohemian masters at Prague University became the leading proponents of this opinion, and they soon found a leader in Master Jan Hus, from 1402 a popular preacher in the Bethlem Chapel in the Prague Old Town. Hus had early inclined to the teaching of the English thinker John Wyclif who claimed that the church would not voluntarily give up its secular wealth and political influence and that only the state and its representatives were capable of compelling it to follow the apostolic life. These critical ideas voiced by university scholars soon found a powerful response both at the royal Bohemian court and among the nobility, and among a much broader range of the population.

1402 Jan Hus preaches in the Bethlem Chapel

Hus's proposals were naturally opposed by the church prelates, and by many of the German townspeople whose numbers and position had been weakened by the plague and the increasing Czech influence in the larger towns. The Germans living in Bohemia began to fear the rise of the Czech element, and this was one of reasons behind the lack of support for Hus from the German scholars at Prague University. In 1409 Wenceslas IV intervened in the disputes at the university by issuing the Decree of Kutná hora, which in practice put the Prague university in the hands of Hus's group. In protest the German teachers and students left Prague and founded a university in Leipzig.

■ In 1414 Jan Hus accepted an invitation to the church council in the imperial city of Constance, hoping that he could persuade a gathering of learned men, who were also striving for the reform of Christendom that his ideas were correct. He was mistaken, since on specific issues the views of the council and of the Hus group were diametrically opposed. Soon after arriving in Constance Hus was arrested, condemned in an inquisition trial and on the 6th of July 1415 burned as a heretic. Not quite a year later, on the 30th of May 1416, Hus's friend Jerome of Prague met the same fate in Constance. Both men were venerated as martyrs by their supporters, to whom their opponents gave the name Hussites.

■ The disgraceful death of Hus and Jerome increased the tension between the Hussite and Catholic sides in the Czech Lands. On the 30th of July 1419 the revolutionary storm broke when the Hussite radicals in the Prague New Town hurled the hated members of the Town Council from a window (the so-called "First Defenestration of Prague"). When Wenceslas IV died a few days later, the Hussite revolution could no longer be contained. It gradually gripped the whole Kingdom of Bohemia (in which the catholics were defending themselves for dear life), while the so-called "adjacent countries" with a predominance of German population, set themselves against it. In Moravia conditions were more complex: part of the nobility joined the Hussite side in the hope of furthering their political and economic interests, but the larger towns, mainly German in population, took up an anti-Hussite position.

■ All the Hussites recognised a common programme known as the Four Articles of Prague, formulated in the Spring of 1420. These articles briefly summarised the basic principles of Hussite teaching on the reform of the church and society in the spirit of God's law (1. to give the laity equality with the priesthood at the mass by allowing all to receive both the blood and body of Christ – hence the label

6th July 1415
Jan Hus burnt
at the stake
in Constance

30th July 1419
Outbreak of the
Hussite Revolution

"In both kinds", Calixtins or Utraquists; 2. Free preaching of the Word of God; 3. Confiscation of the secular property of the church and the exclusion of church influence from secular politics.; 4. The punishment of mortal sins that prevent Christians attaining salvation. The Hussite priests intended to compel not only all the inhabitants of the Lands of Bohemian Crown, but the whole Christian world, to respect these principles. So ambitious an aim, however, was beyond the capabilities of the Hussite revolutionaries.

■ Disputes among the Hussites themselves also created barriers to success. Despite agreement with the programme of the Four Articles, the Hussites split into several doctrinal movements. These ranged from the moderates (part of the Hussite nobility, the university intelligentsia) to the centrists (most Praguers and their supporters in Boehmia) to the radicals, of whom the most important were two unions: the East Bohemian and the Taborite.

■ In 1420, the Taborites even set up their own community of Tábor in South Bohemia, in which they intended to be governed only by the authority of the Bible.

■ Christian Europe regarded the Hussites as heretics and tried to break them by military force. These attempts were led by the Papal Curia, the King of the Romans and Hungarian Lands Sigismund, brother of Wenceslas IV and heir to the Bohemian throne but rejected by the Hussites, and supporters of the Conciliar Movement. In the course of the years 1420–1431 they organised five crusades against Hussite Bohemia, but all ended in failure. The first crusade came to nought outside Prague in the summer of 1420, since it was unable to take Vítkov Hill (today Žižkov), which was

14th July 1420
Battle of Vítkov

Jan Žižka at the head of his army.

defended by the famous Hussite general, Jan Žižkov of Trocnov (d. 11th October 1424). Other expeditions met with defeat at Německý (today Hlavlíčkův) Brod at the beginning of 1422, at the South Bohemian towns of Tachov and Stříbro in 1427 in 1427, and in 1431 not far from Domažlice. The third expedition announced in 1422 never actually mustered. In addition, the Hussites repulsed the intervention of Saxon and Thuringian forces on the 16th of June 1426 at the Battle of Ústí nad Labem.

■ King (and from 1433 Emperor) Sigismund was left with no alternative but to negotiate with the Hussites and consider their demands. A council meeting in Basle also tried to negotiate a solution from 1431. A Hussite delegation headed by the Taborite leader Prokop Holý came to the council in January 1433 to negotiate on the Four Articles, but the discussions dragged on and continued alternately in Prague and Basle. The economic problems of a country exhausted by war weakened the position of the unyielding Taborites and East-Bohemian Hussites. They were opposed by the moderate Hussites who were trying to reach agreement with the council, and who in alliance with the Bohemian Catholics defeated them on the 30th of May 1434 in a battle near the Central Bohemian village of Lipany. Prokop Holý was one of those who fell, and the defeat of the radicals opened the way to an agreement between the Hussites, the Council of Basle and Sigismund of Luxemburg.

■ Its text contained the stipulations known as the Compacts, formally announced in Jihlava on the 5th of July 1436. Essentially the Compacts meant the limited victory of the Hussite programme. Adult inhabitants of the Kingdom of Bohemia and Moravia could choose either the Hussite or Catholic faith. The Hussite Church was considered to be an autonomous part of the Church of Rome, but this proved problematic since unlike the Council, the Pope never recognised the Compacts. Sigismund (d. 9th December 1437), ascended the Bohemian throne, but was forced to agree to the confiscation of the secular property of the church, the representation of the towns and lower nobility in the Land Diet and the exclusion of prelates from that body. With this agreement the Hussite Revolution ended in 1436.

■ The relationship between the Catholic rulers and the Hussites who constituted 70% of the population not surprisingly ran into difficulties. On the 2nd of March 1458, therefore, the Bohemian Diet elected George of Poděbrady, the noble leader of the Hussite Party, as King. It was an exceptional event in Bohemian history since it placed the crown on the head of a man who was not of the dynastic line

1433
Hussite delegation attends the Council of Basle

30th May 1434
Defeat of the Hussite radicals at the Battle of Lipany

5th July 1436
Announcement of the Compacts

2nd March 1458
George of Poděbrady elected Bohemian King

*Western European
image of a Hussite
battle*

and who was regarded by almost all Europe as a heretic.
George of Poděbrady strove to be a good ruler of the "double
people" (i.e. Hussites and Catholics), and to improve his
reputation abroad. In 1464, as part of this policy, he
proposed a plan for a peace union of European rulers which
in many ways foreshadows the principle of the modern UN
organisation. European monarchs, however, rejected the
plan, and George remained isolated at a period when the
Pope declared the Compacts to be void and called on
Christians to wage a new war against the Hussites. Czech
Catholics exploited papal support as did the Hungarian King
Matthias Corvinus, who fought against George for three
years (1468–1471) with varying success. The Lusatian,
Silesian, Moravian and Bohemian Catholic Estates elected

*View of Prague
in 1493.*

**1485
The Religious
Peace
of Kutná hora**

**1517
The St. Wenceslas
Agreement**

Matthias as King of Bohemia in Olomouc in 1469, but after
George's death (22nd March 1471), the supporters of the
"Hussite King" respected his wish and gave the throne to the
Polish Prince Vladislav Jagellion.

■   Double rule in the lands of the Bohemian Crown
ended with the death of Matthias Corvinus in 1490.
Vladislav consolidated all the joint lands under his sceptre
and also became king of Hungary. In 1485 at a diet in Kutná
hora the Czech Catholic estates acknowledged the
Compacts as the fundamental law of the land and concluded
a religious peace with the Hussites, later prolonged "for all
time". After a stormy period Bohemia became a region of
religious tolerance, although this was of course a tolerance
born of necessity, since political leaders were aware that
after a long period of revolution, when Bohemia had lost up
to 40% of its population and was struggling with economic
problems, the state needed tranquillity.

■   We cannot, however, speak of overall stability, since
after the dampening of dispute in the religious sphere, there
was a practically immediate deterioriation in relations
between the royal cities and the nobility, i.e. between the
groups that had gained the most in the Hussite period. Their
twenty-year struggle ended in 1517 with the compromise
known as the St. Wenceslas Agreement. The towns
relinquished several medieval privileges (e.g. the market right
and right to brew beer), while the nobility had to accept the
towns' representation in the Diet. Thus Bohemia came to
have a constitutional structure in which the ruler shared
political power with the Estates (two noble estates, known
as the lords and the knights, and one estate composed of the
royal towns). This model was shared, despite various local
differences, with neighbouring states.

■ The estates model was soon, however, to face a difficult test. On the 29th of August 1526 King Ludwig Jagellion perished in the Battle of Mohács Field against the Turks in Hungary. On the 23rd of October 1526 the Bohemian estates elected the Austrian Archduke Ferdinand I, a member of the Habsburg Dynasty, as king. He soon acquired the Hungarian throne as well, and in this way the Habsburgs crowned their political rise, since Ferdinand's brother Charles V was the King (and from 1530 the Emperor) of the Holy Roman Empire of the German Nation, and also King of Spain. Ferdinand I was a skilful politician striving to strengthen central royal power and weaken the influence of the Estates. He relied on an effective bureaucracy which he entrusted to offices subject to his personal control, and he supported the Catholic Church against the Utraquist Church and the new reformationary churches (the Lutherans and later Calvinists), as well as the church known as the Unity of the Brethren that had emerged in Bohemia around 1460 on the basis of the ideas of Petr Chelčický. In 1556 Ferdinand invited the Jesuit Order, vanguard of the militant Catholicism reborn at the Council

Ferdinand I.

Feast for the Order of the Golden Fleece in Prague in 1585, with Emperor Rudolf II to the left at the table.

1575
The Bohemian Confession

1609
Publication of Rudolf's Letter of Majesty

of Trent, into the Bohemian Lands. Filling the Archbishopric of Prague, vacant in the 15th Century, was another aspect of Counter-reformationary policy.

■   The centralising measures of Ferdinand I and his successors came into conflict with the determined efforts of the Bohemian, Moravian and Silesian Estates to maintain their crucial political influence. This conflict found expression both on the political level (in 1547 Ferdinand I suppressed a rebellion of the Bohemian nobles and townspeople), and on the religious level, as the Estates tried to extract a confirmation of confessional freedoms from the Habsburgs. The Austrian Habsburgs with their rich Catholic relations in Spain hesitated, but in 1575 Maximilan II gave verbal consent to the text of what was known as the Bohemian Confession. This was not confirmed in written form until 1609, in the Letter of Majesty of Emperor and King Rudolf II. In this document a piously Catholic and eccentric monarch, acting against his own conscience, legalised in the Bohemian Kingdom a degree of religious freedom unparalleled elsewhere in the Europe of the time.

■   Rudolf II (1576–1611) has also entered history as an art collector, and patron of artists, writers and scientists (the astronomers Tycho de Brahe and Johannes Keppler worked in Prague in his reign), and frequently also of crooks trying to exploit his generosity. It was in the reign of Rudolf II, the last Habsburg to make Prague his residence, that Bohemia fully domesticated the Renaissance style that had been spreading into Central Europe from Italy. At the beginning of the 17th Century, however, it was gradually squeezed out by a new movement, Mannerism, foreshadowing the rise of the Baroque.

■   Surprisingly, the issue of Rudolf's Letter of Majesty did not calm the situation. The militant Catholic party regarded it as a defeat since it diminished hopes for the development of a centrally controlled central European Habsburg state consisting of the Lands of the Bohemian Crown, the Austrian Lands and Hungary, much of which was at that time under the control of the Ottoman Turks. The tension between the evangelical Estates and the Catholics came to a climax on the 23rd of May 1618, when a group of opposition nobles, dissatisfied with the policy of the Bohemian regents (high officials representing the king), burst into the Prague castle and threw two pro-Habsburg officials (Vilém Slavata of Chlum and Jaroslav Bořit of Martinice) from a window. The victims survived uninjured, but that was irrelevant. The conflict between the Bohemian non-Catholic Estates and the Habsburgs erupted in full force and, as a result of the entanglement of great power interests with the Protestant and Catholic causes, grew into the long-term European armed conflict known as the Thirty Years War (1618–1648).

■   The Bohemian Estates, however, were more or less isolated when they embarked on rebellion, and this was to have fatal consequences for them. They launched their rebellion with some success, electing as king the imperial prince Frederick of the Palatinate, son-in-law of James I of

23rd May 1618
Defenestration in Prague and beginning of the Thirty Years War

8th November 1620
Battle of the White Mountain

Brno around 1600

Albrecht of Valdštejn (Wallenstein).

England, but that was all. Soon conditions changed. On the 8th of November 1620 the Estates army, formed of various mercenaries, suffered a defeat at a small battle on the White Mountain in front of Prague, and its commanders had no intention of defending the capital. Frederick of the Palatinate fled the country and the Habsburgs triumphed. Nothing now prevented the bigoted Ferdinand II from punishing the rebels, and he started to implement his programme of building an absolute monarchy controlled by himself and his closest advisors. Ferdinand's first steps made it clear that the model of the Estates constitution had finally collapsed.

**1627–1628
The Renewed
Land Rule**

■ Those leaders of the Estates Rebellion who had not gone into exile were arrested, and 27 were executed as public examples in Prague Old Town Square on the 21st of June 1621. The king confiscated the estates of all the other rebels in Bohemia, Moravia and Silesia. The authorities started a systematic process of recatholicisation culminating in the issue of a new constitution, called the "Renewed Land Constitution", which came into force in 1627 in the Kingdom of Bohemia and a year later in Moravia. All members of the community of the Estates (i.e. nobles and townsmen) who wished to adhere to a non-Catholic faith had to leave the Czech Lands. The serfs had no choice but to stay, and to accept Catholicism whether or not they wanted it. The constitution declared the Bohemian throne to be a hereditary possession of the Habsburg dynasty, the spiritual Estate took its place in the Diet (while the towns were left with only one vote), and German was given equal status with Czech. As a result of the issue of the new constition and its executive decrees, tens of thousands of people emigrated from the Czech Lands, among them much of the intelligentsia including the father of modern educational theory Jan Amos Komenský (Comenius) (1592–1670). Recatholicisation took place relatively quickly and successfully, and so the Saxon and Swedish forces that entered Bohemian and Moravian territory during the Thirty Years Way, did not gain the support of the population.

■   One famous protagonist in the Thirty Years War was the Czech general and entrepreneur Albrecht of Valdštejn (often known as Wallenstein thanks to Schiller's play), the Commander-in-Chief of the Habsburg forces. After he quarrelled with the emperor, he became the focus of the hopes of leaders of the Czech exiles and the anti-Habsburg powers (Sweden and France). Ferdinand II saw through Valdštejn's game, however, and gave the order to eliminate him. On the 25th of February 1634 the general and his colleagues were murdered in Cheb. His death meant further confiscations and large-scale transfers of property to supporters of the Habsburgs. After the Thirty Years War, which ended in 1648 after the Swedish forces made a hopeless attempt to capture Prague, almost half the noble property in Bohemia was held by members of foreign aristocratic families. It is indisputable that the number of nationally conscious Czech nobles fell, and this was necessarily reflected in subsequent political and cultural development.

■   The Thirty Years War left in its wake a devastated

**25th February 1634
Murder of Albrecht
of Valdštejn
in Cheb**

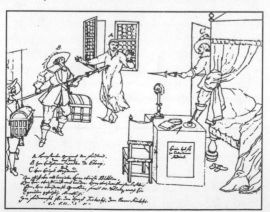

*The murder
of Albrecht
of Valdštejn.*

Jan Amos Komenský (or Comenius, 1592–1670), "the teacher of nations".

1680
Great Peasant Rebellion

Baroque art in the Czech Lands

economy and a population reduced by roughly a third. The road out of decline was to be long and painful. The serf farmers had to pay high taxes, but above all they were bound to the land (they could not move without the consent of the lord and had to carry out compulsory labour duties on the lord's lands). Although in Bohemia and Moravia this system never took such oppressive forms as in Russia or Poland, the peasants were never reconciled to it and rebelled against in on several occasions, most notably in 1690. The most onerous conditions lasted until the early 18th Century, and then the economy in the villages and towns began to recover.

■ One sign of reviving prosperity were the numberous town houses and farmhouses built in the Baroque style which put down roots in the Czech Lands after the Thirty Years War. The Baroque shaped the appearance of Bohemian towns and villages for several centuries. The most characteristic buildings of Baroque architecture are, however, churches and monasteries, noble seats (chateaux and palaces with what were known as French parks), and various practical buildings such as granaries and hospitals. The most distinguished Baroque architects in Bohemia included K. I. Dienstenhofer and J. B. Santini-Aichl, sculptors included the outstanding Ferdinand Brokof and M. B. Braun (both contributed to the gallery of sculptures on Charles Bridge), and the ranks of painters boasted Petr Brandl, Karel Škréta and V. V. Reiner. The Bohemian and Moravian musical Baroque won European-wide fame, and the music of Adam Michna or F. X. Brixi is still played today, together with hundreds of works by lesser known composers. The Czech Baroque could even claim its own saint, John of Nepomuk, who was canonised in 1729 in the last wave of the Counter-Reformationary zeal.

■   At the turn of the 17th/18th Century, the centralised absolutist Habsburg Monarchy had become a great European power, thanks largely to military successes. It encompassed the Bohemian Crown Lands (now without the two Lusatias, which Saxony had gained in 1635), the Austrian Lands, Hungary from which the Turks were retreating, and other territories. A major rival to the Habsburgs was emerging, however, in the form of the Prussia of the belligerent King Frederick II, who wanted to annex the industrially advanced Silesia on the excuse that he did not recognise the hereditary rights of Marie Teresie (1740–1780). In the long War of the Austrian Succession (1741–1748), partly fought on Bohemian territory, he succeeded in his plans. The subsequent Seven Years War (1756–1763) failed to reverse Prussian possession of the greater part of Silesia and Klodzko.

■   Defeat in the struggles with Prussia showed up the outdated aspects of centralised absolutism. Marie Teresie therefore departed from the policy of her predecessors and tried to remodel the Habsburg state in a spirit of emlightenment principles, in order to catch up with the advanced European powers such as England and France. Enlightenment reforms included the creation of a network of schools (compulsory schooling introduced in 1774),

1741–1748
War of the Austrian Succession; loss of most of Silesia

1781
Patent abolishing serfdom in Bohemia

Patent on feudal labour

Josef II(1741-1790)
distributing alms
in Prague in 1772
during a major
famine.

administrative reorganisation (the Empress abolished the Bohemian Court Office - a measure which in practice put an end to the formal vestiges of Bohemian state independence), and emphasis on the development of agricultural and industrial production. After the loss of most of Silesia, the Czech Lands were supposed to become the industrial foundation of the monarchy, while the Hungarian Lands were to specialise in agriculture. The enlightenment reforms culminated on the 13th of October 1781 with the issue of the Patent of Toleration, which legalised the Lutheran, Calvinist and Orthodox faiths, and on the 1st of

November 1781 with the Patent on the Abolition of Serfdom in Bohemia, Moravia and the remnant of Silesia (compulsory feudal labour was not abolished until the revolutionary year of 1848). The great peasant rebellion of 1775 played a major part in securing this reform. The publication of both these important acts was linked with the name of Josef II (1780–1790), son of Marie Theresie.

■ The enlightenment reforms were directed by a state that took little account of the specific features of the different parts of the multi-ethnic Habsburg Empire. Such an approach, combined with the insensitive introduction of German as official language and curtailment of Bohemian traditions, stimulated the growth of Czech national consciousness and the first phase in the formation of the modern Czech nation. This process, which began in the late 18th Century and continued up to the 1870s, is traditionally

Turn of the 18th/19th Century
Beginnings of the Czech National Revival

The Revolution of 1848: the Whitsun Uprising in June 1848.

called the *national revival*. The original efforts of the revivalists to raise the level of the Czech language and forge a Czech national culture in the full modern sense of the word unconsciously contained a political subtext. The cultural emancipation of the Czech nation, which had been deprived of its specific political identity in the course of the 17th and 18th Century, necessarily foreshadowed strivings for the renewal of Czech statehood. In the earlier 19th Century conditions were not favourable for such aspirations. After the Napoleonic Wars, which had affected Czech and Moravian territory (Napoleon's famous victory over the Russian and Austrian armies on the 2nd of December 1805 at Slavkov in Southern Moravia), the absolutist Austrian regime hardened in its attitude to experiments in national emancipation and clamped down on them effectively. Nor were the hopes of the revivalists fulfilled even by the revolutionary year of 1848, when Czech leaders first emerged with comprehensive political demands. These were proposals for the reform of the Habsburg Empire on federalist principles which would respect the rights of the Slav nations (a doctrine known as "Austroslavism"). The dissolution of the meeting of Imperial Diet in Kroměříž in Moravia (7th May 1849), the issue of the Enforced Constitution, punitive measures against opposition leaders (the internment of the popular journalist Karel Kavlíček Borovský in Brixen in the South Tyrol) and curtailment of the activities of revivalist cultural institutions

**1848
Revolutionary
Events in Bohemia**

*Prince Klement
Metternich
(1773–1859).*

such as the Prague National Museum founded in 1818 and the Czech Matice Foundation set up in 1831, all frustrated these dreams. The repressive political atmosphere in 1849–59 (known as the period of Bachian Absolutism), did not, however, hamper economic activity. In the later 19th Century the Czech Lands became one of the most industrial regions of Central Europe. Concerns like the Vitkovice Ironworks, the Škoda Factory in Plzeň or the Plzeň Town Brewery became household names. Sugar refinement became the pride of Czech industry in the period. An unusually dense railway network linked Bohemia and Moravia with Europe and individual industrial centres in the Czech Lands. Outside

Industrialisation of the Czech Lands

The National Theatre.

Prague, industrial production became concentrated in the Ostrava and Kladno regions (coal-mining and smelting), Brno (machine-tool production), northern Bohemia (glass-making) and north-eastern Bohemia (textiles). The rapid industrial development of the Krušné Foothills (coal mines and chemicals), associated with the devastation of the countryside, started at the end of the 19th Century.

■　　It was only with the relaxation of conditions after 1860, when Emperor Franz Josef II formally abandoned absolutism and the Habsburg Empre set out on the road to the creation of a civic society, that Czech political strivings revived. A strong additional impulse was given by the issue of the February Constitution on the 26th of February 1861,

Old Czechs and Young Czechs – the first Czech political parties

which was the basis for the first elections to land diets and the Imperial Council in Vienna, parliament of the whole Habsburg state. The Czech national party was headed by the historian František Palacký (1798–1876), author of the monumental History of the Czech Nation in Bohemia and Moravia, and his son-in-law František Ladislav Rieger (181 801 903). Their cautious if prudent policy did not satisfy the more radical circles in Czech society known as the Young Czechs (who founded their own political party on the 25th of December 1874). Essentially, however, Palacký and Rieger's "Old Czechs" and the "Young Czechs" were united in their efforts to renew Czech statehood and achieve the transformation of the Habsburg Empire into a federation of its historical components.

■   After 1866, when Austria suffered another serious defeat in war with Bismarck's Prussia (the Battle of Hradec Králové on the 3rd of July 1866), conditions seemed favourable for the realisation of such a plan. In 1867 the government in Vienna gave way to Hungarian pressure and agreed to change the previously centralised state into Austria-Hungary (the system known as "dualism"). This equalisation of constitutional rights encouraged Czech politicians to start a broad campaign for the recognition of Bohemian constitutional rights and the extension of dualism to create an Austrian-Hungarian-Czech triadism. Huge meetings took place over almost three years (one of the most famous was held on the occasion of the laying of the foundation stone of the Prague National Theatre in May 1868), but their hopes were disappointed. Hungarian opposition wrecked the dream of Bohemian political autonomy within the Habsburg Empire, even though its principles were formulated in 1871 in what were known as the Fundamental Articles.

■   Failure in the constitutional struggle was to affect the face of Czech politics in the following decades. Bitterness was generated by the fact that the political status of the Czech nation did not correspond to its very rapid economic and cultural advance. In the interest of pushing through their constituional demands, Czech political leaders kept trying to change tactics right up to the outbreak of the First World War, and alternated between a pragmatic loyalism to Vienna and radical nationalist attitudes that roused the opposition of the ethnic Germans who made up roughly a third of the population and feared for their position. The relationship between Czechs and Germans in a single state took on ever more confrontational aspects.

■   In the last decade of the 19th Century Czech society had almost all the features of a modern advanced society. The

1867
Austro-Hungarian
dualism

end of the 19th
Century
The emergence of
new Czech parties

structure of political parties corresponded to a complex social hierarchy. After 1890 the traditional Old Czechs, Young Czechs and the workers' Czechoslovak Social Democratic Party founded in 1878, were joined by the Christian Socialist, National Social and Agrarian parties, and also the small but influential Realist Party led by the university professor T. G. Masaryk. In the 1907 elections, the first to be held on the basis of universal suffrage, the Agrarian Party and the Social Democrats won the most votes.

■   In the cultural sphere, a romantic nationalism had been traditionally dominant since the beginning of the revival. Even before 1900, however, modern movements expressing the changed position of the individual in an over-technologised industrial situation were starting to make on impact on Czech art. At the same time Czech culture was opening up to the world and enjoying great successes, especially in music (the words of Antonín Dvořák, and later the operas of Leoš Janáček) and painting (the worok of Alfonse Mucha in France). Prague Art Nouveau became a byword.

■   The shots fired by the assassin Gavrilo Princip in Sarajevo on 28th June 1914 put an end not only to the life of the heir to the Habsburg throne, Franz Ferdinand d'Este, but also to a whole epoch. The First World War, for which the assassination was the immediate trigger, devastated all Europe, and shook the continent's entire system of values. It undermined the old social order in every European country and provided the opportunity for new social groups to increase in influence. The depleted ranks of the old elites were reinforced by people enriched by the war; in employment and even in public life women started to take the place of the men who had been called to arms; the power of the politically radicalized masses and the people who led them increased unexpectedly. The Bolshevik Revolution in Russia showed where these tendencies could lead. The changes sweeping Central and Southern Europe were likewise wide-reaching in significance. Germany became a republic, and the peoples living on the territories of the Austro-Hungarian monarchy created their own states – the so-called "successor states". Among these new- born states was Czechoslovakia.

■   Before the war the representatives of the Czech people had not striven for full political independence. They had realised that however ill-disposed the Austrian state to Slavs, it created a necessary shield in an area where the interests of Germany and Russia were likely to come into conflict. But the Habsburg monarchy, which had fallen into ever deeper dependence on the German Reich, especially

The First World War and its Consequences

Change in the Attitude of the Czech People to the Monarchy

during the war, was ceasing to fulfil this role. The loss of lives in a war which the Czechs did not regard as their own, economic difficulties, the growing favouritism shown towards German and Hungarians, and the mounting police persecution of the Czech people, all served only to increase discontent. The Czech people's relationship to the monarchy deterioriated sharply.

■ In the end Czech hopes came to be invested in waht was known as "action abroad". Its moving spirit was Professor Tomáš Garrigue Masaryk (1850-1937), who emigrated in 1915 in order to organise the struggle against Austria-Hungary and to gain support among the Allies for the concept of an independent Czech, or as it turned out, Czechoslovak state. His National Czechoslovak Council, in which his efforts were joined by those of the political scientist Edvard Beneš (1884-1948) and the Slovak astronomer Milan Rastislav Štefánik (1880-1919), an officer in the French airforce, relied on expatriate societies and especially on the legions. These were military units composed mainly of Czech (and to a lesser extent of Slovak) prisoners of war and deserters who had decided to wrench independence from Austria by armed struggle. The legions had formed in France and Italy, and chiefly, of course, in Russia where they later became – thanks to their control of the Trans-Siberian Railway – an important element of the unsuccessful anti-Soviet intervention.

■ For a long time, however, it remained unclear whether the Western Allies would respond to the recommendations of the National Council. At first, the allies still hoped for long-term benefits from the Habsburg monarchy, which could, they believed, continue to form a sufficient counterweight to the German colossus. They started to take a more favourable view of the Central European and Balkan nationalist movements only after the Russian revolution of February 1917. The Russian example had shown the potential weakness of the ancient monarchies. This encouraged them to see independent national states as the best barrier against the threat of Bolshevism.

■ The actions of domestic politicians were co-ordinated by the National Committee, a body to which all the Czech political parties sent delegates in numbers proportionate to their results in the last general elections of 1911. As the representative of the interests of the entire nation the National Committee aspired to take on the role of partner to the organs of state. From the summer of 1918 it was also preparing to take control of them. The state, which by that time was simply awaiting its own overthrow, did not

The Beginnings of the Czech Resistance Abroad. Masaryk, Beneš, Štefánik

28th October, 1918

interfere. Even the last Habsburg emperor Karl, whose greatest fear was of the suffering which might be caused by civil war, did not stand in the way of the Czech efforts. He could at least hope that the newly constituted Czech state would not break off all its ties with the monarchy. On the streets of Prague, however, such hopes were already doomed.

Preparations for Taking Power

■ When, on 27th October 1918, the Austro-Hungarian Foreign Minister Julius Andrássy sent a note to the United States in which his government even promised to recognise the rights of Czechoslovaks and Southern Slavs in its attempt to end the war at any cost, the executive board of the National Committee realised that the time had come. On 28th October the National Committee took over the provisioning headquarters, the Grain Office, and later other offices including the Governor's Office. In the afternoon, on Wenceslas Square, independence was officially declared.

The Principle Motto is Order and Prosperity

■ It was clear to the National Committee, and all the other bodies linked to it, that independence was not just a matter of declarations, but a state to be worked for and sustained. It adopted, as its guiding principle, the view that in the chaos of Central European conditions, where the dangers of war and revolution continued to loom large, the new state must create an island of order and prosperity. This aim was made easier to achieve by the fact that despite the clear break with the monarchy in the area of constitutional law the National Committee left all existing laws in force and took over the whole administrative apparatus. At the beginning it could also rely on the fact that even unpopular measures would meet with the agreement of the overwhelming majority of an enthusiastic Czech population.

German Irredentism

■ The major problem for the development of the young state was the initial absence of international recognition for its borders. The integrity of the country's core, the Czech Lands, was menaced even at the very beginning by the decision of the Germans living in the Czech and Moravian border areas, and in Silesia, to establish four separate provinces which declared themselves parts of the Austrian state. Just like the Czechs, the Germans were forgetting all their political differences and taking united action. Their actions, which they justified by appeal to the principle of national self-determination, obviously created insuperable obstacles of a purely practical kind. Separation from the interior caused serious economic and especially provisioning difficulties. At the same time the victorious superpowers had no interest in meeting the members of a defeated people half-way. The National Committee was well aware of all these factors, and when the Germans refused to submit to its authority, it sent military forces to occupy the provinces in November and December of 1918. On 4th March 1919, the day when the Austrian parliament went into session, there were clashes between the local population and the military in the border areas. These cost the lives of more than 50 people. Czech-German relations, already complicated enough, were now burdened with yet another cause of resentment.

■ The border in the Těšín area was also uncertain. In this area Poland, too, was staking a claim. Agreement could not be reached and even military actions did not bring a final decision. The two states finally divided the disputed territory in the face of great-power intervention.

Dispute with Poland

■ Czech domestic and exiled politicians had regarded the creation of a common state with the Slovaks as essential. This had been the only way of ensuring its Slavonic character. In the circumstances, the representatives of the Slovak nation had also accepted this solution as the best one. The Slovaks, living in the northern area of the Hungarian state (i.e. the Hungarian part of the Austo-Hungarian Monarchy) had been exposed to quite strong Hungarianising pressure in the second half of the 19th century. Contacts with the representatives of Czech political and cultural life constituted the only effective support for them.

Slovakia 1918

■ In Pittsburgh, on May 30th 1918, Czech and Slovak expatriate societies had decided to set up a joint state in a form allowing for extensive Slovak autonomy. Slovak representives at home had declared themselves in favour of a joint future with the Czechs only in the Martin Declaration, accepted on 30th October 1918 in Turčanský Svatý Martin. However, those who voted for it had no power to implement their ideas. On 4th November 1918, therefore, the National Committee nominated a provisional Slovak government headed by the Slovak politician Vavro Šrobár. At first Šrobár was unable to prevail against the opposition of the representatives of the old regime and the Hungarian army; he only succeeded in asserting his authority with the help of the Czechoslovak army which, at the turn of 1918/1919, occupied Slovakia up to the demarcation line. This had been created more or less in accordance with Czechoslovak needs on the Danube.

■ In line with the will of the Ruthenian people, and with the agreement of the great powers, Sub-Carpathian Ukraine was also annexed to the Czechoslovak state.

■ The Czechoslovak borders were confirmed by the

Confirmation of the Borders

peace treaties (at Versailles – 28th June 1919, Saint-Germain – 10th September 1919, and Trianon – 4th June 1920), which the allied powers concluded with the defeated states at the Paris Peace Conference. The victorious powers endeavoured, for the most part, to meet the demands of Czechoslovakia, which had been submitted by the most important member of its delegation, Edvard Beneš. It is not surprising that Czechoslovakia became a supporter of the new international order which, on the basis of the results of the 1st World War, was called the Versailles System.

The Ideas on which Czechoslovakia was Founded

■ The beginnings of the independent Czechoslovak state were influenced by liberal democratic ideals originally derived fron the legacy of the French and American revolutions. On 14th November 1918 the National Committee declared itself to be a Revolutionary National Assembly which had deposed the Habsburg dynasty from the Czech throne, and proclaimed the new state a republic. At the same time it abolished noble titles and approved a law on an eight-hour working day. Tomáš Garrigue Masaryk was unanimously elected President of the Republic. The universal authority which he enjoyed, and the fact that he had bound himself to no political party, allowed him, as head of state, to fulfill the irreplaceable role of a non-partisan, integrating figure and exemplary national symbol.

T. G. Masaryk

■ Tomáš Garrigue Masaryk was convinced that "democracy is the political form of humanity". In his view, the justification of the new state lay in Czechoslovakia's potential to realise humane ideals. He exhorted all its citizens to strive for this aim: "All citizens of good will, without distinction of condition, religion or nationality, have been given the opportunity to build an exemplary democratic state, whose task will be to care for the interests of the whole free self-governing citizenry."

The Constitution of 1920

■ The creation of the Czechoslovak legal and governmental system culminated in the constitution approved on 29th February, 1920. Its text, which included a charter of the rights and liberties of the citizen, was principally based on the constitutions of the USA and France. The Language Law, which was passed at the same time as the constitution, guaranteed to minorities the right to use their own language. In practice nothing changed in the life of the largest and most important – German – minority. In particular, there was no abolition of German schooling possibilities in the Czechoslovak Republic. Despite this, it was subjectively very difficult for the Germans to come to terms with the new situation, which brought an unexpected loss of prestige. The Language Law

*Tomáš Garrigue Masaryk (1850-1937). His central
contribution to the founding of the Czechoslovak Republic was
rewarded with the title "President Liberator".*

granted precedence to the Czechoslovak language, which
was proclaimed the official language.

■　　　This reflected the specific ideology of the ČSR –
Czechoslovakism – which conceived the Czech and Slovak
peoples as a single whole. It was an expedient political
construction based on the extreme similarity of the
languages (every Czech can understand Slovak without
being taught, and vice versa), but it glossed over the differences arising from separate histories and cultures.

■　　　In the economic field, however, the gulf which
separated the Czech Lands on the one hand from Slovakia
and Sub-Carpathian Ukraine on the other could not be

Czechoslovakism

**The Economic
Situation**

ignored. The Czech Lands were parts of what was industrially the most developed area in Central Europe. Here, in addition to such traditional industries as textile or glass production, there was a developing machine-tool industry, including automobile and aircraft works, electrical engineering, coal-mining, and shoe manufactures. A highly developed agriculture, often exploiting the advantage of cooperative organisation, had created the basis for a vigorous food industry. The undeveloped manufacturing industry in the eastern part of the country was far from measuring up to this economic level.

Differences between the Czech Lands and Slovakia/Sub-Carpathian Russia

■ Other differences were linked to the economic imbalance. While Czech society was characterised by considerable social and political differentiation, the Slovak people was much more homogeneous and was mainly composed of the rural population. It was particularly lacking in an educated and affluent middle class, since people of this kind had taken over the language and way of life of the ruling Hungarian elites. (For example, of the 400 people who were engaged in literature and journalism on Slovak territory before the war, only 19 declared themselves to be of Slovak nationality – 334 declared themselves Hungarian and 47 German.) Nor could the Slovaks, unlike the Czechs, draw strength from an earlier tradition of independent statehood. Of all the institutions in Slovakia the Catholic church enjoyed the greatest respect, while in the Czech Lands its influence was continuing to decline.

Economic Policy

■ The Czechoslovak state made efforts to assist progress in Slovakia and Sub-Carpathian Ukraine. It focused on increasing literacy and promoting the development of the educational system, and on improving conditions in the area of health and communications. These policies met with considerable success, but the differences between Czechs and Slovaks did not greatly diminish.

Currency Reform

■ Economic policy, implemented particularly by Finance Minister Alois Rašín, was principally directed to freeing the country from the inflationary trend in Central Europe. Currency reform and the separation of a Czechoslovak currency from the Austro-Hungarian currency (involving the stamping of original Austro-Hungarian banknotes and the withdrawal of approximately 1/3 of money in circulation), which was carried out in February and March of 1919, ensured a long-term high exchange rate for the crown. Together with economies in state expenditure these measures contributed to the maintenance of economic stability. On the other hand, this approach inhibited investment activity.

■ On April 16th, 1919, a law on land reform was passed by which all land holdings exceeding 250 hectares were confiscated with compensation and sold to small agricultural producers. The land reform helped to strengthen the position of the Agrarian Party which had drafted it, and also led to a diminution of social conflict in the villages.

Land Reform 1919

■ It proved impossible to calm the social situation in the towns in a comparable way. One factor contributing to the radicalisation of the workers, who were suffering from the post- war disruption of the economy, was agitation by those returnees from the war who had become enthusiastic about Bolshevik ideals in Soviet Russia. A similar effect was produced by news of the proclamation of the Slovak Republic of Soviets which was created on 16th June 1919 in East Slovakia under the direct ideological and military influence of the Hungarian Republic of Soviets. The Slovak Republic of Soviets relied on the support of the Hungarian Red Army, and fell after its retreat on 7th July 1919. Nevertheless, for a short time it seemed that the vision of a socialist revolution which would shake the whole world was being fulfilled.

Radicalisation of the Working Class

■ Demands for sweeping social change were also expressed in the large number of votes cast for the Czech and German Social Democratic parties in the elections of June 1919 (local elections) and April 1920 (parliamentary elections). From the turn of 1919/20, however, both these parties experienced a split between their right and their much larger left wings. The government created by the social democratic Vlastimil Tusar from representatives of his own party and the Agrarian Party, proved unable to function under these circumstances, and resigned. A quarrel over party property sharpened the confrontation between the two factions. The left wing, which was defeated in the dispute, declared a general strike on 10th December 1920. Although the strike did not spread to the whole country, it developed with unexpected ferocity, and in some places turned into an open struggle for power. These challenges were, however, firmly suppressed by the authorities, and those responsible were put on trial. This defeat contributed to a further radicalisation of the left wing, which at a Constituent Congress on 14th – 16th May 1921 proclaimed itself the Communist Party of Czechoslovakia (KSČ). In the Autumn of 1921, the communist parties of the other nationalities of the Czechoslovak Republic (ČSR) merged with it. The KSČ did not, therefore, follow the pattern of the majority of communist parties and develop from a small revolutionary core. On the contrary, it developed as a mass party from the beginning.

The Split in the Social Democratic Movement. Establishment fo the Czechoslovak Communist Party 1921

The National Coalition

■ The split in the Social Democratic Party, and subsequently in all the other workers' organisations, shattered the influence both of this party and of the organised working class. Henceforward it would be principally the parties of the centre and the right which determined the fortunes of the state. After a year during which there was a caretaker government, responsibility for the state was taken over on 7th October 1922 by an all-party coalition government composed of all the main Czech parties and representatives of the Slovak people. Antonín Švehla, head of the Agrarian Party, took on the post of Prime Minister. From this time until the end of the Republic it was a post held exclusively by members of this, the strongest of the Czech parties, which through fusion with the National and Farmers' Party gained a certain amount of representation even in Slovakia and Sub-Carpathian Ukraine. The Agrarian Party brought together the greater part of the rural population, to which it could offer a dense network of co-operatives and other economic facilities. It also gained a significant influence among all categories of clerical workers and state empoyees. Its major partner was the Czechoslovak People's Party, whose supporters were principally recruited from the Catholic population in Moravia. The National Democratic Party was also keen to participate in government. The links between this party and industrial and financial circles, however, created obstacles to its cooperation with the Agrarians, who pursued their own economic policy. Even the socialist parties did not give up participation in government. The Social Democrats gradually recovered from the fiasco of 1920, drawing strength from the largest trades union federation – the Czechoslovak Trade Union Association. The National Socialists were supported by Sokol (the largest physical education organisation) and the legionaries' organisations. From 1923–1935 Edvard Beneš worked in this party.

Czech Parties
Opposition Parties
Loyal German Parties

■ Basic opposition both to any government and to the state as such naturally became the position of the Communist Party (KSČ), which relayed the directives of the Moscow Communist International into the republic. The opposition standpoint taken by the strongest Slovak party – Hlinka's Slovak People's Party, made a conspicuous imprint on relations between the Czech and Slovak peoples. The remarkable influence of the party on the very devout Slovak population derived from its unambiguously Catholic orientation. Its popularity was further increased by the fact that it demanded autonomy for Slovakia from the Prague

Franz Kafka
(1883-1924)

government. The German National Party (Deutsche Nationalpartei - DNP), and especially the German National Socialist Workers Party (Deutsche national-sozialistische Arbeiterpartei - DNSAP), which was based on the same ideological sources and traditions as Hitler's NSDAP, never reconciled themselves to the existence of Czechoslovakia. The other German parties, however, reassessed their original negative attitude. In 1926 the German Agrarian Party and Christian Social Party joined the government, and in the 1930s they were followed by the German Social Democrats. After this, members of the German national minority (for example the Social Democrat Ludwig Czech or the Agrarian Franz Spina) occupied a place in every Czechoslovak government. The National Democrats, who had been trying to counteract the decline in their influence by stepping up nationalist agitation, left the government in protest against the alliance between the Agrarians and the German civic parties. The Socialists also went into opposition to this government, which under the leadership of Švehla represented a strengthening of the position of the bourgeoisie.

■　　　One of the effects of the calming of the political

The Economic Situation in the Period of Prosperity

situation was a favourable economic trend from the mid- 1920s. The majority of indices of prouction and living standards placed Czechoslovakia in 10th to 15th position in the world. In comparison with 1913, the volume of industrial production at the end of the 1920s had increased by 20%. As in all other industrially developed countries, electrification, assembly-line production and work rationalisation made progress in Czechoslovakia. These processes reached their high point in the factories of the "European Ford" – Tomáš Baťa, the Zlín shoe manufacturer. The Škoda Works, one of the largest of European arms producers, also maintained a significant position in the Czechoslovak economy. Škoda's chances of success in arms manufacture were increased still more by the investment of French capital.

Culture – Education

■ In the stormy but pluralist atmosphere of the 1920s a new stage in Czech culture began. The cultural upsurge was based on an educational system of high quality, which gradually extended across the entire state. The schools built in Slovakia and Sub- Carpathian Ukraine provided an opportunity for the all-round development of the Slovak and Ruthenian peoples. The high level of Czech science was demonstrated, for example, by the activity of the later Nobel prize-winner (for 1959), Jaroslav Heyrovský, who designed and constructed the first polarograph in 1925. The diffusion of culture was assisted by new technical media: film and radio, which provided popular education in addition to entertainment.

Literature

■ In the 1920s Czech literature began to gain recognition on a worldwide basis. Credit for this was due especially to the writer and playwright Karel Čapek (who, incidentally, was the first to use the word "robot") and Jaroslav Hašek, creator of the Good Soldier Schweik. Writers, who according to prevailing opinion represented the "conscience of the nation", considered it their duty to come to the defence of humanist and democratic values. This commitment was characteristic not only of Karel Čapek but also, for example, of the journalist and writer Ferdinand Peroutka and the critic F. X. Šalda. Many authors did not hide their social feelings and leftist views; these included the leading creator of social poetry, Jiří Wolker and, for example, Jaroslav Seifert. The poet Vítězslav Nezval, together with Karel Teige, the many-sided theoretician of a range of artistic disciplines, created a new artistic and especially literary movement – poetism. Poetism was a particular Czech variant of surrealism, with which it later merged. Besides those with a leftwing ideological orientation, there were successful writers who were moulded by their v religious faith, such as Jaroslav Durych and Jan Zahradníček. The Czech literary and artistic scene was also greatly enriched by the Liberated Theatre of Jiří Voskovec and Jan Werich.

Prague German-Jewish Literature

■ Prague German (or to be precise, German-Jewish) culture was weakened by the death of Franz Kafka in 1924, and Rainer Maria Rilke in 1926, and by the departure of Franz Werfel. Continuity with earlier development was then ensured particularly by Max Brod and the journalist Egon Erwin Kisch. They were joined by other authors such as Johannes Urzidil. German culture could draw strength from two universities, a multitude of publishing houses and newspapers and an ample network of schools, museums and theatres.

Art. Music

■ Of the modern movements in art it was principally cubism which put down roots in Bohemia. The movement found expression not only in painting but also in architecture and the decorative arts. Cubism fascinated many painters. Even those who later created their own independent style - like Václav Špála, Josef Čapek or Jan Zrzavý - went through a cubist stage. Another identifiable movement which had an impact on Czech painting was surrealism, as is evident in the work of Jindřich Štyrský, Josef Šíma or Toyen (Marie Čermínová). Monumental sculpture was developed on the basis of the older Czech tradition, but important Czech sculptors, such as Jan Štursa and especially Josef Mařatka, also learned from the legacy of Auguste Rodin. European art was enriched by Czech architecture, which was linked with the work of Adolf Loos, Le Corbusier and the Bauhaus Circle. The construction of new public buildings and the creation of integrated town complexes (for example at Hradec Králové and Zlín) in the spirit of constructivism and functionalism provided architects such as Josef Gočár, Pavel Janák, Karel Honzík, Josef Havlíček and F. L. Gahur with a wide range of opportunities to display their talents. It was perhaps Czech music, represented at this period by such composers as Leoš Janáček, Bohuslav Martinů and Josef Suk, that won the greatest international acclaim. Jaroslav Ježek, who most impressed himself on public awareness with the songs which he composed for the Liberated Theatre, also wrote classical music.

Bolshevisation of the KSČ 1929

■ The prosperity achieved in conditions of national independence confirmed the overwhelming majority of the Czech population in the conviction that the road on which they had set out at the end of the war was the correct one.

Even among members of the Communist Party, which took up a position of absolute hostility to the post-war developments in Central Europe, some doubts began to grow about the perspectives of their own movement. As a result of the conflict between dogma and reality the party fell, in 1928, into a deep crisis. The Communist International, which had for some time been pushing through a policy of the Bolshevisation of all communist parties, i.e. their unconditional subordination to Moscow centre, exploited this situation. In the subsequent conflicts it supported the young, ambitious functionary Klement Gottwald, whose opinions precisely reflected the official line of the Comintern. The party was seriously damaged when Klement Gottwald gained the leadership at the 5th Congress of February 18th – 23rd, 1929. It lost a considerable number of members and voters (including a large group of intellectuals) who rejected Gottwald because of his dogmatic views and the way that he had elbowed his way to the head of the party.

The Economic Crisis at the Beginning of the 1930s Growth of Nationalism in the ČSR

■ The conspicuous weakening of the Communist Party did not last long. This was above all because of the Great Economic Depression, which brought yet another period of major social conflicts. In Czechoslovakia the effects of the crisis were delayed until 1930 and peaked in 1932. Industrial production in the ČSR fell by 40%, and other branches of the economy were only a little less gravely affected. The consequences of the crisis for Czechoslovakia were considerably exacerbated by the export character of its economy, because similarly affected countries defended themselves against imports with high tariffs. The most oppressive consequence of the crisis was unemployment. In 1932 the number of unemeployed reached one million according to official statistics, and in reality it was probably 25% higher. The crisis, and therefore the unemployment, primarily affected light industry in the German border areas. The fall in the price of agricultural products seriously affected the Slovak population as well. This was fertile soil for the growth of a nationalistic mood. But even the Czech population demonstrated its dissatisfaction. The government reacted equally uncompromisingly, but was unable to prevent the growth of social and political tension and the radicalisation of both the left and the right wing. On all sides there was a growing feeling that the crisis meant the end of a free liberal economy, and that lessons were to be drawn from this fact for the organisation of society as well. Democracy in the form in which it had hitherto existed seemed outdated, weak and ineffective. The remedy for its ailments was believed to lie in more radical state intervention in all spheres of social life. The government, headed by František Udržal after the death of A. Švehla and from 1932 by Jan Malypetr, tried to master the economic situation, but without significant results. Regulation was recommended principally by the Socialists, who once again entered the government in 1929.

■ In addition to the communists, fascists and nationalist extremists also fought against democratic forms of government. Czech fascism remained confined to the fringe of the political scene. Organisations like the National Fascist Body could not be taken too seriously. The National Union, created in April 1935 by the merger of the National Democrats with various fascist groups, played a more important role. Nevertheless, not even this organisation gained major influence. In Slovakia, on the other hand, Hlinka's Slovak People's Party, which no longer hid its opposition to the Czechoslovak state, gained ever more support.

■ The most serious threat arose from developments in the German minority. In 1933 the activities of the German National Party and the German National Socialist Workers' Party were halted on the grounds of their links with organisations in Nazi Germany and of subversion of the Republic. Their supporters, headed by the hitherto politically inactive Konrád Henlein, then formed the Sudeten German Patriotic Front on 2nd October 1933 (from 1935 this became the Sudeten German Party – Sudetendeutsche Partei, SdP). At first this new party did not take up a hostile attitude to the state and there could therefore be no objections to its existence. Soon, however, its leadership was infiltrated by Nazis who made it, with Henlein's connivance, into a "fifth column" for Hitler. It gradually swallowed the other parties representing the German middle class and even took voters from the German Social Democrats and Communists.

Rise of the Sudetendeutsche Partei

■ In these circumstances the importance of external security increased. In the 1920s the greatest threat to Czechoslovakia had been the demands of Hungary for the revision of the Versailles System. The so-called "Little Entente", a system of agreements between Czechoslovakia, Yugoslavia and Rumania, was aimed at countering such pressure. But differing economic interests meant that the Little Entente could not be really cemented. On 25th January 1924 Czechoslovakia had concluded another treaty with what was then the strongest European state – France. The significance of this treaty increased enormously in January 1933 when the Nazis, who did not hide their aggressive intentions, took power in Germany. The main architect of Czechoslovak foreign policy, Edvard Beneš, realised the

Foreign Policy of the ČSR in the 1920s and 1930s

danger to which the republic was now exposed. French power had declined since the period following the First World War. As soon as the French, in 1929, started to build a system of fortifications on the Franco-German border – the Maginot Line – it had become clear that France was not planning offensive moves against Germany. Yet only a determined attack by French forces, tying up the maximum of German forces, could save Czechoslovakia in the case of a German assault. Beneš therefore redoubled his efforts in the League of Nations, of which Czechoslovakia was a founder member, and encouraged the plan of collective security which the Soviet Union had been putting forward in the League. In the framework provided by closer relations between France and the USSR, a Czechoslovak-Soviet Treaty was signed on May 16th 1935, by which the Soviet Union promised to come to the aid of Czechoslovakia if France did likewise.

■ The democratic public in the ČSR reacted to the growing threat with increasing resolve and a mood of strong antifascism. Mounting expenditure on the armed forces and the construction of border fortifications was accepted with understanding. One important turning-point was the election of the President of the Republic after Masaryk's abdication in 1935. After complex negotiations he was succeeded on 18th December, 1935 by Edvard Beneš, an expression of continuity with earlier policy. As was appropriate to his ability and ambitions, this internationally recognised politician took over responsibility for the entire state.

■ The hostility of Germany was increased by the fact that the ČSR accepted all anti-fascist emigrants – just as it had accepted refugees from Russia and the Ukraine in the 1920s. Not only unknown and ordinary people but also many outstanding representatives of German culture found a refuge in Czechoslovakia. Thomas and Heinrich Mann were given Czechoslovak state citizenship. Others who obtained asylum in the ČSR included the writers Lion Feuchtwanger, Arnold Zweig, Bertold Brecht and Jakob Wassermann, and the painter Oskar Kokoschka. The former German chancellor Philipp Scheidemann wrote a large part of his memoirs in Czechoslovak exile. In the course of 1937 Czechoslovakia found itself ever more internationally isolated. The Western powers failed to react firmly to the actions with which Hitler was testing their resolve. At best they never managed more than purely verbal protests. In practice they were operating a policy of appeasement – of concessions and conciliation – in the hope that Germany would direct its expansionist aims toward the East. In this

Determination to Defend the Country Diplomatic Isolation of the ČSR

The Munich Agreement decided the fate of Czechoslovakia.

hope they were not – at least for a time – mistaken. The first independent state to be seized by Hitler was Austria, in March 1938. This extended the Czechoslovak border with Germany, and the new sector was not protected by fortifications. The encirclement of Czechoslovakia was nearly complete... It was above all the SdP, playing the role of spokesman for all Sudeten Germans, that functioned as Hitler's tool for the liquidation of the ČSR. Beneš and the Czechoslovak government, after 5th November headed by Milan Hodža, tried to solve all the problems by compromise. Berlin, however, ordered Henlein to keep stepping up his demands and not to accept a compromise at any price. The solution of the Sudeten problem was to be nothing less than the destruction of Czechoslovakia. This situation was exploited promptly by Hlinka's Slovak People's Party, which acted with ever increasing self-confidence.

■ All was not yet lost, and an energetic assertion of the strength of the whole international coalition would have stopped Hitler. The principal aim of France and Great Britain was, however, to avoid a war for which, despite numerous warnings, they were not preparing. Both countries therefore put heavy pressure on Czechoslovakia. They wanted the crisis

Pressure on the ČSR The Munich Agreement, 29th September 1938 The Second Republic

to be resolved to the satisfaction of Adolf Hitler and at the expense of the friendly state whose security France had guaranteed. One aspect of this pressure was the mission of Lord Walter Runciman, who visited Czechoslovakia from the end of August to the beginning of September. His expert opinion, that Czechs and Germans could not live together in a single state, was based on information provided for him by his Sudeten German hosts. It nevertheless became one of the principles of the strategy of the Western powers, which offered Hitler the amputation of the border areas of Czechoslovakia and their annexation to Germany. This solution was finally sealed by the Munich Agreement, concluded on the night of 29th – 30th September, 1938, between the representatives of Italy (Benito Mussolini), Germany (Adolf Hitler), France (Edouard Daladier) and Great Britain (Neville Chamberlain). Up to the last minute Czechoslovakia wanted to defend itself. This determination was evident in the two mobilisations declared on 20th May and 23rd September 1938. Both mobilisations found a unanimously enthusiastic response among the Czechoslovak population. Democratically inclined citizens of German origin also came to the support of the republic. But Czechoslovakia alone, deserted by its allies, could not sustain a direct confrontation with Germany. President Beneš, negotiating under time constraints and extraordinary pressure, therefore decided to exceed his constitutional authority and to accept the conditions dictated on his own responsibility, without parliamentary assent. On 5th October 1938 Edvard Beneš abdicated and on 22nd October he flew to Great Britain.

■ Munich left its imprint on the nation, creating an ingrained distrust for the Western Allies and long-term deep depression at Czechoslovakia's own weakness. The trauma arising from this defeat without a fight was to afflict society and its political representatives no less oppressively than the results of any defeat in battle.

Acceptance of the Munich Diktat

■ In accepting the Munich Diktat Czechoslovakia undertook to withdraw from the territory settled by Sudeten Germans, where Nazi terror broke out immediately after its annexation to the Reich. In the following months Czechoslovakia had then to accede to the territorial demands of Poland (in the Těšín and Spiš regions), and Hungary (in the southern area of Slovakia and Sub-Carpathian Russia) as well. The Republic thus lost its border fortifications, an important area of coal deposits, part of its light industry and several railway junctions. The overall area of the state was reduced by perhaps a third. Under these circumstances the Republic could no longer defend itself at all or even consider an independent foreign policy. It could try to preserve at leat some internal autonomy but even this was difficult. Capitulation to Hitler had encouraged extremist elements, hostile to democracy. A significant proportion of the Czech public began to have doubts about the democratic organisation of society.

■ Hlinka's Slovak People's Party exploited the opportunity of the weakening of the state and, on 6th October, together with other Slovak civic parties, publicly demanded autonomy for Slovakia. The very next day, 7th October, saw the establishment of the first Slovak autonomous government, headed by Josef Tiso. Subsequently a Sub-Carpathian autonomous government was established as well. These changes were confirmed on 19th November by a law on the autonomy of Slovakia and Sub- Carpathian Ukraine. The states' official name then became Czecho- Slovakia. On 30th November, Emil Hácha, hitherto Chairman of the Supreme Administrative Court, was elected President of this modified state.

Czecho-Slovakia

■ The new political situation demanded extensive changes in the organisation of public life. In view of the critical economic situation policies aimed at enhancing state authority, and limiting individual privileges and liberties, were mainly accepted. The right and centre parties combined to create a Party of National Unity, whose leader, the former Agrarian Rudolf Beran, became Prime Minister. The Social Democrats and *some* of the National Socialists formed a National Labour Party. The activities of the KSČ were first suspended and later entirely prohibited – but the party was not subjected to persecution. The parliamentary character of democracy suffered its greatest blow with the so called Authorisation Law, which allowed the government, for a two-year period, to substitute its own decrees for the existing laws and even to change the constitution by decree.

Changes in Internal Organisation

■ Czecho-Slovakia tried to maintain the best possible relations with Germany. This policy, followed especially by the Minister of Foreign Affairs František Chvalovský, did not, however, find an adequate response. Hitler was not interested in good relations with Czecho-Slovakia, but in controlling the country. To this end he used the efforts of the Slovak separatists, who with the assistance of their shock-troops – the Hlinka Guards – gained the uper hand in Slovak politics. On 14th March, 1939, the Slovak Autonomous Assembly, in accordance with Hitler's demands, proclaimed an independent Slovak state. (One of the first steps taken by this state was the expulsion of the Czech population from the country.)

■ Hácha, accompanied by Chvalkovský, was then,

The German Occupation, 15th March 1939

The arrival of the German forces in Brno, 15th of March 1939.

during a visit to Berlin, forced to accept the German decision. On 15th March 1939, the German army occupied the Czech Lands and on 16th March the occupiers proclaimed the Protectorate of Bohemia and Moravia.

■ An edict issued by Hitler on 16th March 1939 guaranteed the Protectorate autonomy and its own government. No decision, however, could be allowed to threaten the interests of the Reich. The Protectorate did not have its own diplomatic representation abroad, and its armed forces – the government army – could only fulfil auxiliary tasks. Since only one party – the National Union – was permitted, parliament did not exist. Emil Hácha, as State President, stood with the government at the head of the Protectorate, but real power was in the hands of the Reichsprotektor and his Office, where the Sudeten German Karl Hermann Frank occupied the key position. The Germans controlled the Protectorate administration through lower bodies – landrats – and all the German security and police organisations were active on the territory of the Protectorate – especially the Sicherheitsdienst and the Gestapo. They were looking for all opponents of the "new order" among the ranks of the Czech and German population. The German emigrants were their first targets, although the majority of these had managed to escape before 15th March 1939.

Establishment of the Protectorate of Bohemia and Moravia, 16th March 1939 Nazi Policy in the Protectorate

■ Not long after the establishment of the Protectorate the antisemitic Nuremburg Laws began to be applied there. The "Aryanising" Germans seized Jewish property, and October 1941 saw the beginning of the "Final Solution" to the Jewish question, i.e. the transport of Jews to extermination camps. Between 1941 and 1945, 73,603 Jews went through the transit camp for the Jewish population sited in the town of Terezín, which became notorious as the "gateway to death". It was envisaged that the Czechs, too, would later be exterminated, resettled or Germanised. But during the war the Germans needed the Protectorate principally as a secure hinterland reliably fulfilling industrial and arms production requirements. The Germans introduced the principles of a planned economy into the Protectorate and its entire economy was subjected to German supervision and war aims. German concerns acquired capital shares in the Czech enterprises which interested them, a development facilitated by the imposed exchange rate of 10 crowns to the mark.

The "Final Solution" of the Jewish Question

■ For the Czech population the occupation meant yet another shock, and yet more humiliation. On the other hand, it provoked even greater indignation and the determination not to give in to pressure. The nation found encouragement particularly in the field of culture – in the poets Jaroslav

Czech Culture

Seifert, František Halas and Vladimír Holan, and the essays of Václav Černý. In an atmosphere of general danger interest rose in works which recalled the certainties of national life – the native landscape, motherland, history. All these works, for example Vladislav Vančura's Pictures from History, were really also polemics against the Nazi propaganda which emphasised the dependence of Czech cultural development on German traditions. Theatre performances and concerts of Czech classical music expressed the same striving for reassurance.

17th November 1939. Closure of the Czech Universities

■ The Czech population showed their dissatisfaction by participating in gatherings which marked various national celebrations. There was a clearly political dimension to the demonstration held on 28th October 1939 to mark the anniversary of the founding of Czechoslovakia. During this demonstration Jan Opletal, a student of medicine, died after being shot by a German policeman. The occupying forces used the further demonstrations during his funeral as a pretext for what was hitherto their most brutal act of repression: on 17th November 1939 all Czech institutions of higher education were closed, many students were taken to concentration camps and 9 leaders of the student movement were shot. These measures were meant by the occupiers to break the power of the Czech intelligentsia as leading elements in the nation. At the same time, however, they drew the attention of the whole world to the brutal act. 17th November later became International Students Day.

Beginnings of the Domestic Resistance Resistance Abroad

■ In the Spring of 1939 the first resistance organisations came into existence. The close colleagues of Edvard Beneš formed a Political Headquarters. Active and reserve officers created the Defence of the Nation. Representatives of Czech culture joined together in the Faithful We Remain Petition Committee. In the Spring of 1940 these groups united under a common headquarters, the Central Leadership of the Domestic Resistance (ÚVOD). Despite losses inflicted by the Nazi security apparatus, the Czech resistance managed to achieve some reasonable successes, especially in intelligence activity. The communist resistance developett independently, at first confused by the Soviet-German Pact. It gained a clearer orientation only after Hitler's Germany launched a military attack on the Soviet Union in June 1941. The organisation of resistance abroad proceeded concurrently. The communists had their natural centre in Moscow, while representatives of the other parties, who had succeeded in escaping, began to concentrate in London around Edvard Beneš, who had returned to political life immediately after the occupation of the Czech Lands.

He had some difficulty in asserting himself against his competitors for the leading place in the resistance (especially Milan Hodža and Štefan Osuský). At first, moreover, the governments of France and Great Britain, who stuck by the Munich Agreement, did not wish to activities aimed at the restoration of the Czech Republic. After the defeat of France the Czechoslovak National Committee decided, on 9th July 1940, to create a provisional state structure headed by Beneš as President. Msgr. Jan Šrámek became Prime Minister.

■ After the beginning of the Second World War on September 1st 1939 the military aspect of the resistance came to the fore. The first to experience battle were fugitive Czechoslovak soldiers in Poland, where a Legion of Czechs and Slovaks had been formed. After the defeat of Poland the members of this legion, together with their commander Ludvík Svoboda, were interned in the Soviet Union. They were only able to rejoin the battle in March 1943 in Sokolovo. In France two Czechoslovak infantry regiments were formed, and these were involved in rearguard actions during June 1940. Earlier, citizens of the former ČSR had joined the French Foreign Legion. A group who won themselves quite extraordinary honour were the Czechoslovak pilots who withdrew from Poland and France to Great Britain, where they played a significant part in the Battle of Britain. A Czechoslovak infantry battalion fought in the Middle East alongside the British forces, as later did an anti-aircraft regiment, which from October 1941 to March 1942 and in the first half of 1943 won distinction in the defence of Tobruk.

Czechoslovak Soldiers Abroad

■ Involvement with military operations against Nazi Germany strengthened the position of the Czechoslovak exile community. On 18th July 1941 the Czechoslovak government abroad was definitively recognised by Great Britain and, on the same day, by the USSR. On 30th July the USA followed suit.

■ In the Summer of 1941 the illegal resistance within the Protectorate sprang into greater life. ÚVOD and the new illegal leadership of the KSČ reached agreement on the creation of a joint body – The Central National Revolutionary Committee of Czechoslovakia. The National Revolutionary Intelligentsia Committee was a similar organisation. The number of strikes and acts of sabotage increased. For this reason the Reichsprotektor up to this point, Konstantin von Neurath, was replaced on 27th September 1941 by a specialist in the fight against opposition movements; this was a General in the SS and Police and the Chief of Reich Security Head Office Reinhardt Heydrich. Heydrich immediately ordered the declaration of

Arrival of Reinhard Heydrich in Prague

Massacre of the men in Lidice, 19th of June 1942.

martial law and launched a widespread assault on all illegal organisations. He did not even hesitate to arrest the Chairman of the Protectorate government, General Alois Eliáš (executed on 19th July, 1942) for having contacts with the London exiles. To the policy of intimidation he added social demagoguery, aimed principally at the working classes. In response to Heydrich's offensive, the London government organised an assassination plot against him, carried out on 27th May, 1942 by two parachutists, Jan Kubiš and Jozef Gabčík. It was a feat unparalleled in the entire period of the war. The Nazis reacted to the death of one of the most important men of the Third Reich with a frenzied wave of terror (the Heydrichiad), during which, for example, the villages of Lidice (10th June, 1942) and Ležáky (24th June, 1942) were annihilated. *This* persecution so shattered the forces of the domestic resistance that it recvered its original impetus only toward the end of the war.

The Czechoslovak-Soviet Treaty 1943

■   As soon as it became clear, in the second half of 1943, that the defeat of Nazi Germany was approaching, the superpowers began to give thought to the future organisation of Europe and of individual states. The form of post-war Czechoslovakia was strongly influenced by the Czechoslovak-Soviet Treaty signed on 12th December 1943. The

Treaty linked the post-war fortunes of Czechoslovakia to the USSR as the most important guarantor of Czechoslovak independence. In subsequent conversations with a communist delegation it was decided that there would be extensive regulation of political life and extensive intervention in property relations in the post-war republic. Beneš realised how much stronger the influence of the communists had become both at home and worldwide, and he knew that particularly in Central Europe it would be impossible to ignore them. Like many others he believed that a more sober, democratic policy direction, more concerned with domestic than with foreign problems, would prevail in the USSR after the war. He intended to dampen the revolutionary fervour of the communists at home by bringing them into government and involving them in the solution of concrete problems.

■ In the following year, 1944, the Eastern Front was already moving up within reach of the former eastern borders of Czechoslovakia. The days of the authoritarian clerico-fascist Slovak state, which had fought against Poland and the USSR and found itself in a state of war with the USA, were numbered. Its population, which had lost the original enthusiasm born of independence, had long ago ceased to support it. At the end of 1943 the representatives of the civic resistance (Ján Ursíny, Jozef Lettrich, Vavro Šrobár) and the communists (Gustáv Husák, Karol Šmidke, Laco Novomeský) were moving closer together. On the basis of the so-called Christmas Agreement between the two sides the Slovak National Council (SNR) was established. Its role was to co-ordinate the struggle against the domestic dictatorship and its German sponsors. At the same time, the political programme of the SNR demanded the re-establishment of Czechoslovakia as a joint state of Czechs and Slovaks on the basis of equality of right. The military campaign against the regime was to be designed to fit in with the possibilities and moves of the Red Army. The major force of the uprising was to be the Slovak army. But the first fighting broke out on August 29th, 1944, before all the necessary preparations were complete. At first it proved possible to occupy a relatively extensive territory with a centre in Banská Bystrica, but at the end of October German units, called to assist by the Slovak state, had crushed the uprising. The rebel army therefore had to change over to a partisan mode of warfare. The Slovak National Uprising (as this expression of resistance by the Slovak people was later called) was supported by the Allied Airforce, and the Red Army pushed through the Carpathian Mountains to come to its aid. The 1st Czechoslovak Army Corps, which had taken part in this operation under the aegis

The Slovak National Uprising 1944

of the Soviet forces, set foot on Czechoslovak territory on 6th October 1944.

■   The liberation of the whole of Czechoslovakia, however, and especially of Prague, did not take place until more than half a year later. As in other Moravian and Czech towns, which came out in opposition to the Germans from 1st May, in Prague an uprising broke out on 5th May, once again earlier than had been planned. The German command realised the importance of Prague as a capital city and centre of communications, and therefore ordered that the uprising be suppressed at any cost. The Czech National Council, in which the communist Josef Smrkovský gained a decisive position alongside the non-aligned Professor Albert Pražák, placed itself at the head of the rising and co- operated with military experts. But in no way could it secure sufficient weapons.

■   At first it seemed natural that the Americans, who had already reached the demarcation line in Western Bohemia, would come to the aid of Prague. But the High Command of the Anglo- American forces forbade General George Patton to cross the line, since the Allies feared conflicts with the Soviet Union. On the critical day, May 7th, Vlasov troops intervened on the side of the insurgents. These were originally Russian prisoners-of-war, whom an ex-Soviet commander – General Vlasov, had won over to fight in the war against the USSR on the German side. But they failed to reach agreement with the ČNR and on 8th May started to withdraw from Prague towards the West. On 8th May ČNR representatives and the German General Rudolf Toussaint signed a protocol on capitulation, by the terms of which the fighting was to cease and the Germans allowed to retreat towards the West. But the fighting did not stop. Only on 9th May did units of the Red Army reach Prague, and these helped to clear the city of the remnants of enemy forces. The last shots of the Second World War on European soil were fired south-west of Prague by the small town of Milín on 12th May 1945.

■   The post-war Czechoslovak Republic was not renewed in the form in which it had existed before September 1938. By an agreement between the ČSR and the USSR of 29th June 1945, Sub-Carpathian Ukraine was annexed to the USSR as Transcarpathian Ukraine. The official justification for this change was the result of a plebiscite which the USSR had staged.

■   A still greater change related not to borders, but to the German population of the pre-Munich republic. Anger the Heydrichiad the view took hold in the domestic

The end of the war. Arrival of the Red Army in Prague,
9th May 1945.

resistance movement that there could be no place in the new state for the German minority. This notion was quite consistent with the provisional ideas of the Allies on the reorganisation of the whole Central European region. After some hesitation Beneš added his voice to this plan and finally all political parties approved it. First of all the so-called "uncontrolled transfer", the unregulated expulsion of the Germans from inside the state's borders took place. This was accompanied by a great deal of cruelty, and according to existing estimates 6,500 Sudeten Germans were murdered and perhaps 20,000 died as a result of unceasing exhaustion and suffering. The Potsdam Conference, primarily devoted to deciding the fate of Germany and the Eastern borders of Poland, on 1st August 1945 endorsed the transfer of the German populations from the ČSR, Poland and Hungary. This legalised the so-called "organised transfer". In all approximately 2,700,000 Germans were expelled.

■ The new Czechoslovak government, in which the key posts were occupied by communists, returned to Prague on 10th May. It brought with it a programme named Košice programme, after the place where it had been officially

The Košice Government Programme and the System of People's Democracy

Czechoslovakia and its Neighbours after the Second World War.

proclaimed on 5th April. Its contents, which even President Edvard Beneš supported, expressed a commitment to extensive social changes. Its gradual implementation created the system of so-called "people's democracy", which despite external similarities differed markedly from the pre-Munich parliamentary democracy. Its basis was the creation of a National Front, a union of permitted parties which had shared in the activities of the resistance abroad (Communists, Social Democrats, National Socialists, members of the People's Party; on the Slovak side the Democratic Party and the Slovak Communist Party). The largest pre-war parties – the Agrarians and the Slovak People' Party – were forbidden together with several others. The National Front monopolised the right to political decision-making. Its decisions were binding on all the constituent parts of the political parties – even on the party press and especially on parliamentary deputies. It was thus placed above parliament and outside democratic control.

Nationalisations

■ The material foundation for this development was created by the confiscation of the property of Germans, Hungarians, traitors and collaborators by a presidential decree of 19th May 1945 and also by the nationalisation of the mines and key industries, joint-stock banks, private insurance companies and the food industry on 28th October 1945. Two thirds of the industrial potential of the Republic found itself in state ownership. A presidential decree of 21st June 1946 paved the way for land reform in the course of which the Ministry of Agriculture distributed the land confiscated from Germans, Hungarians and collaborators.

(The so-called Beneš Decrees were issued with the unanimous approval of all political forces and were ultimately approved by parliament. They thus acquired the force of law.) The political atmosphere was also significantly influenced by what were known as the "unified organisations", of which the most important was the Revolutionary Trades Union Movement. These at first appeared to be non-party organisations, but de facto served the interests of the strongest party – the KSČ. These organisations were well suited to bringing pressure to bear through various public campaigns and acts.

■ The policy of the ČSR was further constrained by the necessity of considering the USSR, which had become much more influential in world affairs and especially in Central Europe. The distribution of power in the international arena had, indeed, been confirmed by the superpower conferences at Yalta (4th – 11th February 1945) and Potsdam (17th July – 2nd August 1945).

The International Political Context of Czechoslovak Politics

■ All these circumstances were reflected in the parliamentary elections of 26th May, 1946. Overall the KSČ won 40% of the vote. (The situation in Slovakia, where the Democratic Party won 60% of the vote differed from the overall results for the whole republic and even more from the results in the Czech Lands.) The KSČ used this endorsement of its position to make major advances in the next year. Negotiations concerning the Marshall Plan became the key issue which most clearly revealed the international position of the ČSR, which hoped to fulfil the role of mediator between East and West. The Plan, launched in June 1947 by the US Secretary of State George Marshall, aimed to assist the reconstruction of the European economy. The USSR saw an attempt to threaten the Soviet sphere of influence, and therefore, after initial hesitation, took up a resolutely hostile position against it. Czechoslovakia was interested in the plan, which indeed created the basis of West European prosperity, and was the only state among the Soviet allies to accept an invitation to the conference at which it was to be negotiated. Under pressure from Stalin, however, it withdrew its participation. The way in which this was done was also revealing about conditions in the ČSR. The government decided on so crucial an issue; parliament was merely notified of it.

The Struggle for Democracy. Rejection of the Marshall Plan 1947

■ In the Autumn of 1947 Stalin increased the pressure on the Czechoslovak communists to bring their struggle for control of Czechoslovakia to a victorious conclusion. The communists therefore stepped up their efforts on all fronts, raised demands for further nationalisations, and continued

Communist Preparations for the Seizure of Power

to undermine the non- communist parties, into which they infiltrated their own specialists and professionals from they Ministry of the Interior, and even made unsophisticated assassination attempts. Enforcement of the interests of the Communist Party was also entrusted to the party's shock troops – the People's Militia, ostensibly founded for the defence of factories. Under this assault the non-communist parties, which until that point had been too concerned to pursue their individual policies, united. The Social Democrats, however, did not entirely manage to free themselves from communist influence. Disputes broke out in the National Front, which had hitherto functioned only thanks to the acquiescence of the non- communist parties.

The Communist Coup on February 1948

■   The struggle for power culminated in February 1948. On 20th February 12 ministers from the 3 non-communist parties resigned in protest against the communist advance. They believed that others would join them and that then the communists would either retreat or the government, its credibility shaken, would fall and make way for new elections. They did not, however, ensure that the number of ministers resigning was sufficient to force the whole government to step down. Klement Gottwald exploited the opportunity. By carefully orchestrating political pressure and demonstrations of strength he managed to get the president to accept the resignations. He then filled the vacant posts with people who worked for him in the non-communist parties. On 25th February it was all over. On 2nd June the mortally ill President Beneš abdicated after refusing to put his signature to the constitution drawn up by the communists.

Dictatorship of the Proletariat

■   The February coup divided Czechoslovak society. Some were enthusiastic and convinced that the victory of communism was in harmony with the development and spirit of history. Others suffered the first wave of persecution. Yet others went back into emigration.

■   Within a short time the regime changed into a true dictatorship. The elections were not free, but were nevertheless obligatory, and the independence of the judiciary disappeared. The non-communist parties became mere satellites of the KSČ, whose will they carried out. The state and representative bodies suffered the same fate. The KSČ membership card had conferred privileges and precedence over non-members as early as 1945, but there was of course tight discipline within the party. A group of leading functionaries had the power of decision without having any constitutional or legal responsibility. But even these functionaries were not independent. Their steps were sometimes inspired and always controlled by advisors from the Soviet Union.

■ As the bulwark of the new power, which proclaimed itself the defender of the interests of the working class, 200–250,000 workers were appointed to selected offices. The rest of the population was the target of indoctrination by extensive propaganda. Nor was the development of a security apparatus forgotten. The realisation of the basic aims of the communist movement required the universal liquidation of existing networks of civic rights and liberties.

■ Like all the countries of the socialist camp Czechoslovakia was destined to go through a stage of preventive terror. Officially this was no more than the defence of the revolution from enemies and evil-doers, but in practice it was a matter of terrorising all potential opposition and stirring up visions of general danger. For this reason the question of real guilt played no part in the proceedings, and the secret police themselves often fabricated "crimes". The security forces focused on all groups which did not agree with the regime or which could be considered to have the potential for disagreement.

Political Trials

■ The end of 1948 saw the trial of representatives of the Czechoslovak anti-fascist resistance headed by General Heliodor Píka, who was executed. In May 1950 the biggest post-war political trial started. It was directed against Milada Horáková and her colleagues, and led on to others. Milada Horáková, a national socialist deputy, had been condemned to eight years' imprisonment by the Nazis for her part in the resistance. For the crime of considering ways of opposition to the communist regime she was sentenced to death by a Czechoslovak court and executed on 27th June 1950 despite worldwide protests. Between March 1950 and July 1954 there weve a whole series of trials of Czech and Slovak church dignitaories and believers. The regime regarded the Catholic church, with its traditions and relationships outside the framework of the state, as an especially dangerous enemy.

The Trial of Milada Horáková

■ The political trials ultimately gathered their own momentum and slipped out of the control of their organisers. With the help of Soviet experts a search was launched for enemies within the party's own ranks. This purge ended in the trial of a ring of conspirators against the state led, allegedly, by the former General Secretary of the KSČ – Rudolf Slánský. Among those condemned was even one of the most important of the Slovak communists – Gustáv Husák. In contrast to Slánský and his colleagues he ended in prison and not on the gallows. The total number of victims of communist repression has been estimated at between 200,000 and 280,000.

Reconstruction of the Economy in Line with the Ideas of the USSR and KSČ

■ Immediately after seizing power the communists embarked on the final liquidation of private enterprise. By the end of 1948 more than 95% of the employees in industry were already working in the state sector. The new regime brought the same resolution to bear on the closure of the premises of tradesmen and craftsmen. Even in this area only state or co-operative enterprises were to be allowed fo function. Production and exchange were to be regulated not by market mechanisms but by plans conceived and implemented by a powerful and very large economic bureaucracy. Economic and social development as a whole was to be divided up and arranged into five-year plans.

■ In line with the wishes of the USSR an extensive reconstruction of Czechoslovak industry was set in motion. It was based on the unrealistic conception of Czechoslovakia as a machine-tool superpower. The main emphasis was placed on heavy engineering and arms production. Arms manufacture employed as much as 1/3 of the entire capacity of Czechoslovak industry. The other branches of industry, especially consumer industry, suffered from a lack of resources and were on the verge of collapse. The consequences of artificially accelerated industrialisation had a major impact on agriculture, which was to lose its character as private production and provide the necessary labour force. After two waves of forced collectivisation (1949–1953, 1955–1958), collective farms were operating in 80% of local communities. Despite all the promises, however, agricultural production stagnated.

Further Integration into the Soviet Bloc

■ Grave economic difficulties also resulted from changes in foreign trade. The Soviet Union, and to a lesser extent the other countries of the socialist camp, replaced the developed Western countries as Czechoslovakia's main trading partners. The economic and political dependence of Czechoslovakia on the Soviet Union deepened after the Council for Mutual Economic Assistance (COMECON) on 1st January 1949. The political and especially the military ties between the countries of the eastern bloc were later strengthened still further by the establishment of the Warwaw Pact on 15th May 1955.

Currency Reform and the First Crisis of the System, 1953

■ The state decided to tackle the critical situation with a currency reform declared on 30th May 1953. Every citizen could exchange 300 old crowns for 60 new ones, and the remainder at a rate of 1:50. At the same time the ration coupon system was abolished. These measures devalued savings and reduced living standards. The workers responded to the reform with a series of strikes and demonstrations. In Plzeň army units and the People's Militia had to be called in to suppress a demonstration. The Czechoslovak regime, which after the death of Klement Gottwald on 14th March 1953 was led by Antonín Zápotocký as President and the Party chief Antonín Novotný, was forced to seek some kind of solution. In Moscow, where after the sudden death of Josef Stalin on 5th March, 1953 a new stage of development was slowly beginning, they were advised to develop an internal policy which would take more account of the needs of the population. The forced collectivisation was temporarily suspended, and the brakes were put on heavy industry to the advantage of light industry. Within a short time the economy recovered somewhat.

■　　Another crisis, however, this time political, was looming on the horizon. Once again it was, of course, linked to events in the USSR. Khrushchev's criticism of the "cult of personality", which, at the 20th Congress of the CPSU in February 1956, revealed the extent of Stalin's crimes, could not and was not meant to involve the whole system. Nevertheless, it eroded hitherto unshakeable certainties and was a stimulus to critical thought. The KSČ leadership tried as far as possible to keep Khrushchev's speech a secret, but was unsuccessful. What was originally discussion within the party soon had consequences outside the framework of the KSČ and contributed significantly to activating the whole Czechoslovak public. The most open criticism was heard at the Second Congress of the Writers' Union, on 22nd – 29th April 1956. Despite this the party was able to halt the debates and silence critical voices. Society was still too intimidated by the recent terror and, on the other hand, soothed by the distinct improvement in the economic situation. In these circumstances nobody wished to go too far. For this reason too Czechoslovakia was able to act as a strong bulwark of Soviet policy during the outbreaks of Polish and especially Hungarian resistance.

Consequences of the Twentieth Congress of CPSU, 1956

■　　After the death of Antonín Zápotocký the National Assembly, on 19th November, 1957, elected as President Antonín Novotný, 1st Secretary of the Central Committee of the KSČ, who now embarked on a long period as the most powerful man in the state. In 1960, in order to stress the importance of his government, a new constitution was approved which now contained, among other elements, a passage on the leading role of the KSČ. The claim that the construction of the basis of socialism had already been completed was reflected in the change in the country's name to the Czechoslovak Socialist Republic (ČSSR).

The New Constitution. The Czechoslovak Socialist Republic

■　　The unreality of this view was already manifest in the second year of the 3rd Five-Year Plan, 1961–1962.

Beginnings of Reform Culture in the 1960s

It proved possible to halt the fall in production after a short time, but the five-year plan nevertheless collapsed. It was ever more obvious that a centralised, command economy was not meeting the needs of development. Among economists, led especially by Ota Šik, the idea of linking the plan with the market gained in popularity. Their proposals were then, in emasculated form, taken up as the basis for an economic reform which was to be tested experimentally. Ideological barriers were thus relaxed under pressure of necessity. It was the cultural world that made the most use of the opportunity presented, and refused to submit to ideological demands. Academic and research centres were activated and began to break down dogmatic standpoints especially in relation to national history. A large number of translations of relatively modern philosophical and scientific literature were produced with the aim of filling the gaps in knowledge which arose from the recent period. In the magazines Literary News, Face, and others, the reader could once again find opinions for which only the author stood as guarantor. Artists named the reality to which the others had closed their eyes. The social commitment of the creators of Czech culture reached a peak in the Fourth Writers' Congress in 1967.

■   The Sixties became a golden age of Czech culture. Every work by Milan Kundera, Václav Havel, Bohumil Hrabal or Josef Škvorecký found numberless admirers. Throughout the republic small-form theatres sprung up. These were theatres of poetry and song, which like the most famous of them all – Jiří Suchý and Jiří Šlitr's Semafor Theatre – recreated the informal atmosphere of earlier cabaret. The established classical theatres, for example Otomar Krejča's Theatre Behind the Gate, were just as popular. It was in film, however, that the Czechoslovak culture of the period won most acclaim. The so-called "New Wave", represented by the names of Miloš Forman, Ivan Passer, Jan Němec, Věra Chytilová and Jiří Menzel, won a significant place in the history of cinematic art.

The Situation in Slovakia

■   The situation in Slovakia looked more or less the same. Thanks to the continuous flow of financial resources from the Czech Lands, Slovakia was able to undergo industrialisation on a grand scale. The standard of living in the two parts of the state – at the price of a slowdown in development in the Czech Lands – equalised. Antonín Novotný's anti-Slovak attitudes, however, contributed to a situation in which the longing for an improvement in political conditions was accompanied by explosive demands for a transformation of the relations between the two

Alexandr Dubček greeting participants in the 1st of May Parade, 1968.

nations. For these reasons Slovakia as a whole came to support efforts for reform.

■   It was, indeed, an attack led from Slovakia that proved fateful for the political career of Antonín Novotný. In their criticism of Novotný the Slovak communists therw caution to the winds and in December 1967 already openly called for his removal from the highest office. Novotný could do no more than put off the decision until the beginning of January 1968. At the plenary session of the Central Committee of the KSČ on 3rd – 5th January he capitulated and his place was taken by the more or less compromise candidate Alexander Dubček (1921–1992).

■   For some time it looked as if the change in the leadership would have no larger consequences. But a section of the ruling elite saw in the succession of a younger, relatively unknown but also uncompromised official an opportunity to transform the political system in accordance with its own ideas. This became evident particularly in March, when the appearance of several other politicians (especially Smrkovský and Šik) showed that the reform demands were meeting with support even in the highest places. The media came out in support of the new direction in policy, and helped to create the "Prague Spring" as a period of public (not closed-door) policy. This gave the "process of revival" an exceptional dynamism, and at the same time made any kind of tactical manoeuvring impossible.

■   In such a climate Alexander Dubček was able to work effectively, and his unostentatious performance soon

Emergence of Alexander Dubček in January 1968

The Prague Spring 1968

won him great popularity and genuine mass support. On March 22nd 1968 Antonín Novotný relinquished his remaining office of president and on 30th March the National Assembly elected General Ludvík Svoboda as his successor. Soon after that a large number of high officials were replaced. Oldřich Černík put together a new government and Josef Smrkovský became Chairman of Parliament. The emergence of new organisations (KAN - the Club of Committed Non-Party Members, the K 231 - Club of political prisoners condemned on the basis of paragraph 231) undermined what had hitherto been the organisational monopoly of the communist party and its satellites. In this way the outlines of a new political system called "socialism with a human face" began to appear.

■   The definition of the boundaries of advancing democratisation was the subject of the Action Programme which the Plenary Session of the Central Committee of the KSČ adopted in April 1968. The Action Programme was an attempt to answer the question of how to democratise society to the greatest possible extent while still maintaining the leading role of the Communist Party. The solution suggested was that the party would cease to enforce its decisions through the administration and state power apparatus, but would try instead to persuade the nation that its decisions were the correct ones. Other public organisations would play a greater role and would be guaranteed the right to opposition. In January, when teams of experts were being formed to devise this programme, such ideas sounded radical. Only a quarter of a year later, however, they seemed limited to people who had already grown used to speaking without fear and reading practically uncensored newspapers. Their feelings were expressed by the writer Ludvík Vaculík in his statement, 2,000 Words, published on 27th June 1968. In it he pointed out that so far the changes had affected only the highest positions, and warned that in the municipalities and factories everything was just as it had been before.

The Opposition to the Reforms and their Allies Abroad

■   The Action Programme represented what was perhaps the maximum that the supporters of the old order were willing to accept. In the light of the mass support that Dubček's reform course enjoyed, their opposition did not present too great a danger. What was decisive, however, was that the representatives of the communist movement headed by the Soviet leader Leonid Illyich Brezhnev began to perceive the Czechoslovak reforms in just the same way as the supporters of the old order. The USSR feared for the integrity of its empire, which might perhaps be undermined by contagious thoughts about a socialism no longer based on

August 1968. An unknown man tries to halt a tank with his own body.

the threat of terror. Poland and East Germany reacted no less vigorously. The ČSSR was resistant to diplomatic pressure. Brezhnev finally decided on military intervention.

■ During the night of 20th – 21st September Czechoslovakia the armed forces of the USSR, People's Republic of Bulgaria, Hungarian People's Republic, German Democratic Republic and Polish People's Republic moved in to occupy Czechoslovakia. It proved impossible, however, to form a collaborationist workers' and farmers' government from the domestic enemies of the reform efforts. On 22nd August 1968 the so-called Vysočany Congress of the KSČ met in what was already an illegal assembly, and this took a major share in organising civil resistance to the occupation. The Soviet soldiers, ignored or heaped with reproaches, found themselves quite unable to influence life in the occupied country. At the time the Soviet leaders were

The Soviet Occupation on 21st August 1968

Student demonstration following the death of Jan Palach.

therefore compelled to negotiate with the people whom they wanted to overthrow. During negotiations of 23rd – 26th August they finally succeeded in forcing Dubček, Svoboda, Černík and others to sign the so-called Moscow Protocols, which legalised the presence of the Soviet soldiers in the country. The Czechoslovak leaders hoped that in exchange for this basic concession they would be able to maintain the reformist course at least in the economic sphere.

Developments after August 1968

■   The promises of the reformers were fulfilled, however, only in one respect: on 28th October the federalisation of the Czechoslovak state was announced. Instead of a single government there were now three – federal, Czech, and Slovak. Similarly, a Czech National Council and a Slovak National Council now decided certain issues in addition to the Parliament of the whole state. This was all, however, that the Soviet leaders would allow. Indeed, they did not even abide by the undertakings which they had made in August. With the help of their supporters among Czechs and Slovaks they broke down the unity of the reform forces. It was a process that not even the despairing protest of student Jan Palach, who set fire to himself in Prague's Wenceslas Square on 16th January 1969, could halt. Stormy demonstrations after the victory of the Czechoslovak ice hockey team over the Soviet team on 28th March 1969 were a pretext for further repression. On 17th April 1969, Alexander Dubček was removed from the post of 1st Secretary of the Central Committee of the KSČ, and replaced by Gustáv Husák, who accommodated himself to the situation. After Dubček, other representatives of the Czechoslovak reform movement were also forced to step down. In 1970 all communists were subjected to screening, after which 1/2 million people had to leave the party. The country was hit by yet another wave of mass emigration.

■ Men installed by Moscow gradually came to occupy decision- making posts. Alois Indra became Chairman of the National Assembly, and Lubomír Štrougal became Prime Minister. Major influence in the Presidium of the Central Committee of the KSČ was acquired by Vasil Biľak, who in December 1970, together with Jan Fojtík, submitted a document entitled "Lessons from the Crisis Developments

Gustáv Husák (1913-1991, 1975-89 President of the ČSSR, 1969-87 General Secretary of the KSČ, leading architect of the regime of "normalisation".

in the Party and Society after the Thirteenth Congress of the KSČ". The "Lessons" condemned the Czechoslovak reform of socialism as counter-revolutionary. This interpretation became the official, compulsory version.

"Normalisation" after April 1969. Federalisation

■ A complete return to the situation before January 1968 was not possible. Nevertheless, the new rulers of the ČSSR did all they could to achieve it. Some of those who did not intend to reconcile themselves to the development were made the subject of political trials, but these did not end in executions. Others were unable to escape the constant attentions of the secret police. Opponents of the regime were not allowed to carry on with prestigious professions. As the sole employer the state only allowed them to work where they would not be able to associate with other people – for example as stokers, nightwatchmen etc. Even the children of suspected dissidents were punished since the authorities did not allow them to study. Citizens of the ČSSR were not permitted to travel freely. The centralisation of political decision-making was paralleled by the central planning of the economy. The regime tried to gain support by artificaly maintaining living standards. The population reacted with growing apathy. The depleted ranks of the Communist Party were filled by young people hoping for advancement an a career, but the majority withdrew into their private lives.

Czech Culture Abroad

■ The outside world showed great interest in what survived of independent Czechoslovak culture. Theatres all over the world performed Václav Havel's plays, and the works of Milan Kundera, Bohumil Hrabal, Ivan Klíma and Ludvík Vaculík were translated into many languages. In 1984 Jaroslav Seifert won the Nobel Prize for Literature. Among the film directors who emigrated, Miloš Forman gained the greatest acclaim, while Jiří Menzel and Věra Chytilová gave the most delight to audiences at home. But these were exceptions. Even culture – like other fields – was controlled by people who substituted fidelity to the political line for ability.

Charter 77

■ Society fell into a depression from which there was little movement until the events of 1977. The January 1st of that year saw the publication, in dramatic circumstances in Prague, of the Charter 77 Declaration, which exhorted governing circles in the ČSSR not to violate human rights and thus to fulfil their international obligations. The group which signed the Charter had emerged at the end of 1976. The immediate stimulus to its formation had been given by the acts of protest against the prosecution of members and fans of the rock group Plastic People. Among the Charter signatories were the playwright Václav Havel, the philosopher Jan Patočka, the writers Ludvík Vaculík and

Pavel Kohout, the former "Prague Spring" politicians Jiří Hájek and Zdeněk Mlynář and 252 others. The group brought together representatives of the whole opposition spectrum. The Chartists overcame differences of opinion on individual problems through dialogue conducted in the spirit of tolerance and respect for human rights. The Chartists provided the basis for the gradual formation of an informal civic initiative which regardless of persecution functioned right up to the fall of the communist regime.

■ The Charter gained a greater influence on events in Czechoslovakia in the second half of the 1980s, when it was already becoming clear that socialism could not keep up with the development in the advanced capitalist countries. But the decision-making positions continued to be occupied by the people who had seized power at the beginning of the 1970s. Cosmetic changes – such as the replacement of Gustáv Husák, as General Secretary of the KSČ by Miloš Jakeš in December 1987 – made no difference. The regime had fossilised and had lost the ability to react effectively. The Czechoslovak leadership had watched Gorbachev's policy of perestroika and glasnost with mistrust. It feared that the Soviet reformer would identify himself with the legacy of 1968 and "socialism with a human face", which would challenge the legitimacy of its power. The majority of the Czechoslovak public was waiting for him to do so.

Growth of a mood of opposition

■ Although the policy of the KSČ was officially unchanged, the party's confidence was undermined by the changes in the USSR, to which it had vowed undying loyalty for so many years. On the other side, critical opinion and civic courage was on the rise, and was manifest in demonstrations in August 1998 (the 20th anniversary of the Soviet Invasion), and the beginning of 1989 (the 20th anniversary of the death of Jan Palach), continuing on the 1st of May and the 21st of August of the same year. Repressive measures were no longer enough to quell the opposition movement, but tended simply to add fuel to the flames. Opposition groups and initiatives found an ever more widespread response throughout the population, which was also becoming more sensitive to changes on the international scene. Attention naturally focused on the stormy developments in the USSR, where centrifugal tendencies were already strong, and there was no less interest in the course of reform in Hungary or the results of the elections in Poland, which in the summer produced the first government headed by a non-communist prime minister. The prestige of the only real ally left to communist Czechoslovakia – the GDR, was falling, especially with the exodus of East German

citizens to the West via Prague (i.e. via the West German Embassy in Prague) in September and October, and soon the fate of the East German state was sealed with the mass demonstrations ending in the demolition of the Berlin Wall – the main symbol of the separation of the lands of the Soviet bloc from the free world.

■ Under such circumstances the old regime was unable to hang on even in Czechoslovakia. On Friday 17th November (the 50th anniversary of the execution of nine Czech student leaders and the closure of the universities by the Nazis), a large student demonstration took place, planned with the involvement of members of unofficial groups. In the course of the event, spontaneous expressions of resistance to the repressive regime were met with brutal police intervention and the demonstration was violently broken up. The parallel between the actions of the Nazi and communist security forces provoked a storm of public anger.

17th of November. Beginning of the Velvet Revolution

■ The population began by mass written protests demanding an investigation into the police action, and in some cases revision of government policy. Some sections of the official structures also cautiously but prudently distanced themselves from the violence. These included the Czechoslovak Socialist Party, the Socialist Union of Youth and – what was even more important – their respective daily newspapers, Svobodné slovo and Mladá fronta. Full public declaration of war on the communist regime, however, came only with the strike of students (in universities and to some extent in secondary schools), and theatres, which on Monday 19th November launched what became known as the gentle or "velvet" revolution, characterised not by violence but by its use of the weapons of information and publicity.

■ Two organisations had already emerged to lead the opposition movement on the 18th of November: Civic Forum (OF), and The Public Against Violence (VPN) in Slovakia. They were composed of Charter 77 activists, students and intellectual sympathisers, and gradually attracted other citizens. Although Alexander Dubček and other politicians associated with 1968 returned to public life, it was Václav Havel who took on the role of universally acknowledged authority. In huge demonstrations Czechs and Slovaks let it be known that the overwhelming majority of the people wanted change and the end of one-party government. Some communist leaders tried to force the People's Militia and

OF and VPN

The general strike of the 27th of November 1989 on Wenceslas Square.

army to an armed putsch, but they failed to gain the necessary support. On the contrary, the two-hour general strike on 27th November showed that the population supported the demands of the opposition. Within roughly ten days, the course of future development was decided.

Government of National Understanding. Václav Havel becomes president

■ On December 10th, a government of national understanding was formed and effectively took power. It was headed by Marián Čalfa as Prime Minister and composed of leaders of the opposition movement Civic Forum and The Public Against Violence, non-party figures, members of the smaller political parties and a few representatives of the former ruling communist party who had gone over to the opposition. Under public pressure, the KSČ removed many of its deputies from legislative bodies, and representatives of the new political forces were co-opted in their stead. On 29th December 1989, the transformed National Assembly elected Václav Havel as president.

The first free elections. New laws.

■ Elections to the Federal Assembly and both national councils (the first free parliamentary elections for nearly 45 years) were held on the 8th–9th of June 1990 and definitively confirmed the change of regime. The two main movements won an overwhelming majority, obtaining 170 seats in the 300-member Federal Assembly (divided into the Assembly of Nations and the People's Assembly). Civic Forum gained a convincing victory in the elections to the Czech National Assembly, taking 127 seats while the communist party won 33 seats, the Movement for Self-Governing Democracy – Association for Moravia and Silesia (promoting increased self-government for Moravia) won 22 seats, and the Christian and Democratic Union – Czech People's Party gained 19 seats. Even before the elections, at March, April and May sessions, the assemblies had passed the basic reforms establishing and strengthening a democratic society: laws on civic association and rights of assembly and petition, the placing of all forms of ownership on an equal legal footing, laws on joint-stock companies, enterprise by individuals, economic relations with companies abroad and so forth. The civil and criminal law codes were amended, and the death penalty, for example, was abolished. A law on elementary and middle schools abolished the unified form of school.

Approaches to economic transformation

■ The major focus of attention was change in the economic system. There was no doubt about the need to abandon the socialist model and reintroduce a standard market economy based on private ownership, business enterprise and a competitive environment. The majority of the population was in agreement on this issue, and prepared

Václav Havel (b. 1936)

to accept a temporary drop in living standards. There essentially emerged two schools of thought on economic reform. One group, led by František Vlasák and his colleagues, mostly from the Czech government, recommended a gradualist method involving the restructuring of concerns under state supervision to be followed by privatisation using classic methods. The procedure favoured by this group was applied in the case of the biggest transaction that it initiated – the entry of Volkswagen into the Škoda Automobile Works in Mladá Boleslav. In view of the fact that all the industrial and commercial concerns in Czechoslovakia belonged to the state or were controlled by co-operatives, this approach appeared to be too slow. Moreover, there was a danger of spontaneous and self-serving privatisation of the concerns by their managers, who might deliberately run them into the ground to the benefit of other enterprises, such as their own private firms.

■   The second group of economists therefore prevailed. Led by the Federal Minister of Finance Václav Klaus, it gave precedence to what was known as shock therapy, involving price deregulation (from 1st January 1991), liberalisation of foreign trade, a restrictive govern-

Change in ownership seen as the most important step

ment financial and monetary policy and the introduction of the internal exchangeability of the Czechoslovak crown. Klaus placed the main emphasis on radical and rapid change in ownership, and in February 1990 his circle came up with the unconventional idea of what was known as "coupon privatisation". This idea was that every Czechoslovak citizen could obtain, for a small charge, the opportunity to obtain a "coupon book" allowing him or her to order shares in selected privatised companies. This form of privatisation attracted not only individual citizens, but newly established funds that bought coupon books from private individuals or, more often, promised to use them to generate profits of several times their face value within a certain period. The project, launched on 18th May 1992, met with an unexpectedly strong response, and more than eight and a half million people joined in coupon privatisation. Other properties were included in what was known as "large-scale privatisation", launched on the 1st of October 1991, in which firms were sold to specific buyers either directly or on the basis of public tender. Smaller service and retail firms were earmarked from state property and sold at auction in what was known as the "small privatisation" campaign, started in January 1991. The restitution campaign, designed to return real property appropriated by the communist regime after 25th February to its original owners or their heirs, served a similar purpose with the additional aim of righting wrongs committed by the communist regime. Foreign capital provided a major impulse in the reconstruction of the inadequately or badly structured economy. The involvement of foreign firms provided funds, but also opened up new foreign markets to Czechoslovak firms and provided an opportunity for the transfer of know-how.

■   This scenario of economic reform was generally applauded as highly effective both at home and abroad, and was held up as an example to other states. This route to reform, symbolised by Václav Klaus, enjoyed exceptionally strong political and social support. The pitfalls of the "Czech way" were only to become apparent later.

Czechoslovakia and the world

■   Austria abolished visa obligations for Czechoslovak citizens while the Velvet Revolution was still happening. In 1990 other states followed, especially in Europe. In the euphoria at the fall of communism it appeared that Czechoslovakia would be rapidly and easily welcomed into the community of Western European states. As the complications in the way of European unification multiplied, however, and economic recession deepened, these original hopes cooled. Western European exporters welcomed the

Forms of privatisation

opportunities offered by the Czechoslovak market, but domestic producers, using relatively cheap labour forces, were often faced with barriers in relation to Western markets. Nonetheless, export to the West was becoming a bare necessity for Czechoslovakia, hit as it was by the collapse of markets in Eastern Europe, especially the USSR and the GDR.

■ Czechoslovak foreign policy concentrated on ridding itself of all dependence on the USSR. It contributed to the dissolution of the Warsaw Pact (1st July 1991), and COMECON. On 27th June 1991 the last Soviet soldier left Czechoslovak territory. After 38 years, on 20th September 1990, Czechoslovakia renewed its membership of the International Monetary Fund and the World Bank for Renewal and Development, which it had helped to establish. On February 21st 1990 Czechoslovakia became a member of the Council of Europe and on the 16th of December 1991 it signed an agreement of affiliation to the European Community. "Return to Europe" (entry into the European Union) and NATO remained the fundamental goal. Co-operation between Czechoslovakia, Poland and Hungary as the so-called "Visegrad Three" (named after the meeting of the leaders of the three states in the Hungarian town of Visegrad on the 15th of February 1991), resulted in the signing of the Central European Free Trade Agreement (CEFTA) at the end of 1992.

■ All these fundamental and often unexpected changes were accepted by the population with a fair degree of understanding, and citizens tried hard to adapt to the conditions of the market economy and a democratic society. Their efforts were embodied in the innumerable new businesses founded, as well as foundations and other public initiatives. Despite problems caused by redundancies from unprofitable firms and the curtailment of employment in agriculture, social peace was maintained. The laid-off workers were absorbed by the previously neglected service sector, and unemployment rates were kept to minimal levels. Society began, however, to polarise in terms of both politics and nationality. Civic Forum and The Public Against Violence, both movements that lacked a solid hierarchical structure, were not very well adapted to the regular running of public affairs. The abnormally large number of people supporting these movements itself ruled out the possibility of consensus in all but very general questions, and the logical result was fragmentation. In April 1991, the Civic Democratic Party (ODS), orientated under the leadership of V. Klaus to right-wing voters, broke away from Civic

Population accepts reforms

Splits in OF and VPN

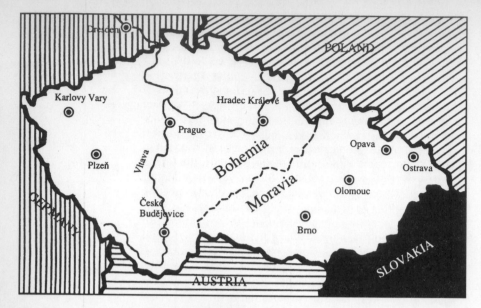

The Czech Republic

Forum as the most powerful fraction, while an incomparably smaller group – the Civic Movement (OH) sought to remain faithful to the original ideals of non-party politics. The Civic Democratic Alliance (ODA), combining defence of Czech interests and conservative values, had split off from OF even earlier.

■　　In Slovakia by contrast, the right -wing party - the Civic Democratic Union - that had emerged from the VPN, enjoyed little electoral support. The majority supported the Movement for a Democratic Slovakia, founded by Vladimír Mečiar, which had split off from VPN when the latter had instigated Mečiar's dismissal from the post of Slovak Prime Minister.

Growing alienation between Czechs and Slovaks

■　　During the November Revolution and the subsequent phase of reconstruction of the political system, the two movements, Civic Forum and the Public Against Violence, had worked as allies, but later they diverged. In the new and freer conditions, the differences in the orientations of the two peoples, or perhaps their political representatives, could emerge more strongly. The first major conflict occurred as early as 1990 in a dispute over the name of the state. The Slovak deputies rejected the president's suggestion for a return to the name, "the Czechoslovak Republic", and an agreement to rename the state, "the Czech and Slovak

Federative Republic" (ČSFR), finally passed on the 20th of April 1990, was reached only after long negotiations. Arguments about the naming of the state would not have been important, however, had they not reflected deeper differences in views of the shared past. A major aggravating factor soon emerged in the form of the different reactions in the two states to economic reforms. In Slovakia they were accepted with much less enthusiasm and with more qualifications than in the Czech Lands. Voices from Slovakia calling for greater independence from Prague did not fail to find a Czech echo. Both national governments, the Czech headed by Petr Pithart and the Slovak led by Vladimír Mečiar, put forward the view that strong republics possessing decision-making instruments would be the best basis for a genuine federation. The national governments also increasingly took over areas of jurisdiction from the federal government, and as their independence of the federation decreased, so too did their distance from each other. The replacement of Mečiar as Slovak Prime Minister by the Christian Democrat Ján Čarnogurský did not halt the trend. The state began to divide, slowly but irreversibly.

■   The run-up to the second parliamentary elections took place in a situation in which calls for radical change in the constitutional relationship between the two states on the basis of confederation, or even full independence for Slovakia, were gaining ever greater support in Slovakia, especially in the circles around Mečiar's Movement for a Democratic Slovakia (HZDS). The Slovak National Party, in particular, pushed strongly for complete independence, while it was generally the right wing in Slovakia that defended the existing system of co-existence. The Czech public rejected the idea of a confederative arrangement, but also generally accepted that Czechs had no right to prevent the Slovak nation from following the road to national sovereignty.

■   In the second parliamentary elections in June 1992, the left emerged the clear victors in Slovakia – the HZDS triumphed and the post-communist Party of the Democratic Left (SDĽ) made significant gains, while the rightist parties – the Democratic Party, the Civic Democratic Union and the Christian Democratic Union – all suffered greater or lesser losses. In the Czech Lands the elections resulted in a convincing win for a right-wing coalition of the strongest party, the Civic Democratic Party, combined with the Civic Democratic Union, and the Christian Democratic Party and Christian and Democratic Union – Czechoslovak People's Party. The Czech left remained divided between the

Constitutional reform or full Slovak independence?

Results of the second parliamentary elections

communist (The Left Bloc, dominated by the Communist Party of Bohemia and Moravia), and the non-communist left, primarily represented by the Czechoslovak Social Democratic Party (the election results are presented in the graph).

Division of Czechoslovakia

■ The divergent results of the elections in the Czech and Slovak Republics reflected the different orientations of the majorities in the two nations and contributed to the decision on the future of the common state. The situation made it impossible for a functioning parliament or viable government to exist. The victors in the elections therefore held a series of meetings in which they decided for the division of the federation. On the 25th of November 1992 the decision was taken to abolish the Czechoslovak Federal Assembly, and on the 16th of December the Czech National Council approved the constitution of an independent Czech state.

Founding of the Czech Republic

■ Despite anxieties, the division (including the division of the currency) took place in an atmosphere of calm and dignity. On the January 1st a new state appeared on the map of Europe – the Czech Republic, with a territory of 78,864 km² and a population of 10,302,000. The last Czechoslovak president, Václav Havel, was elected first president of the Czech Republic on January 26th 1993, and others who had been key figures in the transformation of Czechoslovakia into a parliamentary democracy, especially those who had been architects of economic reform, became leaders of the new Czech Republic. The chairman of the strongest party, Václav Havel, was appointed as Czech Prime Minister.

The ČR in international relations

■ The Czech Republic inherited Czechoslovak membership in the UN, Council of Europe and the OSCE (Organisation for Security and Co-operation in Europe). On 4th October 1993, the Minister of Foreign Affairs Josef Zielenec signed an agreement on affiliation to the European Community and on 28th November, the CR became the 26th member of the OECD. The international prestige of the Czech Republic was also enhanced by visits from heads of state, such as the US President Bill Clinton in January 1994, and Queen Elizabeth II in March 1996, and from Pope John Paul II in April 1997. In 1994 the presidents of seven Central European states met in the East Bohemian town of Litomyšl, and at this informal meeting instigated by V. Havel, clearly indicated their interest in consolidating relations between the countries of the region. Relations between the CR and its largest neighbour – Germany – developed very well; links multiplied in the form of all kinds of projects and programmes of co-operation in economic and cultural fields, and there was an unprecedented boom in private tourism. The two states tried to overcome the problems arising from conflicts in the past with a Joint Czech-German Declaration signed on 21st January 1997.

■ Like Czechoslovakia, the Czech Republic several times expressed its readiness to take its share of responsibility for developments in Europe. In March 1992 Czechoslovakia had sent a military unit to serve as part of the UNPROFOR forces deployed in the former Yugoslavia. Later, on the 29th of November 1995, the Czech government approved the participation of Czech army units in the multinational forces (IFOR) under NATO leadership which were entrusted with supervision of peace-keeping on former Yugoslav territory. Czech soldiers have also been involved in the SFOR mission. The reputation of the CR in the field of international relations is underlined by the fact that from the 1st of January to the 31st of December 1995, it was a temporary member of the UN Security Council.

■ The achievements of Czechs sportsmen and sportswomen have also helped to promote the CR on the international scene. In 1996 and 1999 the Czech ice hockey team won the world championship, and in 1998 it carried off the Olympic Gold Medal at Nagano. In 1996 the Czech football team reached the final of the European Cup. At the Atlanta Olympics, Czech athletes won 4 gold, 3 silver and 4 bronze medals.

■ Culture has found its place in the new conditions, as well, and despite numerous gloomy predictions it has not collapsed in the new economic situation. The successes of Czech film-makers, for example, especially the young generation, have shown their capacity to shine even in fierce international competition. The film "Basic School" by director Jan Svěrák was nominated for an Oscar, and his next film, "Kolya" actually won an Oscar in 1997. The International Film Festival at Karlový vary has consolidated its reputation, and the Prague Spring Music Festival remains a top international musical and social event. The 61st Congress of the PEN Club, held in Prague on the 6th–12th November 1994, was an opportunity to highlight the role of intellectuals in Central and Eastern Europe.

Czech culture in the new era

■ In the field of fine arts, the re-opening of the Prague Trade Exhibition Palace (Veletržní Palác) in December 1995 was an event of the first importance. The permanent exhibition of modern art installed in this 20th-Century architectural monument represents a major step forward, providing the public with a richer and more objective view of Czech artists and artistic movements that were banned or subject to disinterpretation under the former regime. A multitude of recently founded private galleries are facilitating the development of contemporary art of all kinds. In the same way, publishing houses have multiplied, offering the Czech public the chance to read new books from at home and abroad, and works that were previously mutilated by the censor or prohibited altogether. The boom in publishing has also, of course, brought a flood of lower quality, trivial publications.

■ One completely new phenomenon in Czech culture has been the private television station NOVA, which started broadcasting on the 4th of February 1994. Its orientation to the taste of the average viewer has brought it unexpected economic success and, of course, a great deal of criticism for supposedly habituating society to violence and crime. The concentrated diet of American films that it offers has also heightened fears of the Americanisation of Czech society. On the other hand, competition from this go-getting station had undoubtedly forced state television into a greater awareness of its tasks – objective news reporting and the broadcasting of more intelligent programmes.

Social changes

■ Czech society accepted the wide-ranging changes and price shocks that followed the November Revolution in a calm spirit. The government was aware of the importance of the social aspects of reform and the need to keep the population well-informed. The trust that the right-wing government enjoyed was confirmed by local elections held on the 18th–19th of November 1994. The largest number of votes went to ODS, and KDU-ČSL candidates emerged the victors in the small rural communities. The Czech Social Democratic Party (ČSSD) had not yet made much headway. Society was beginning, however, to experience sharp economic and social differentiation. Limited groups of affluent businessmen, managers and officials were emerging, but there was no consolidation or expansion of the middle classes in the sense of smaller businessmen, and members of the intellectual professions. The initial enthusiasm for the post-November changes began to evaporate. A more sober view, also informed by increasing knowledge of the outside world, showed that the transformation had not been as successful as had been claimed.

The first major economic problems

■ The problems appeared first in the health service. On the one hand, in the new conditions Czech medicine could use more effective drugs and better equipment imported from abroad, and so improve the quality of medical care. On the other hand, however, it became apparent that the system based on rating doctors according to quantity of procedures and examinations conducted, and on the operation of an unlimited number of insurance companies, was leading to unchecked growth in financial costs. Many health facilities were in deep financial trouble, and the problems raised questions on the extent to which healthcare could be safely left to market forces. Similar questions relating to the need for state intervention in the economy were raised by a problem that was increasingly evident in the mid-nineties – the growing foreign trade deficit. For a long time the figures were interpreted optimistically, on the assumption that Czech firms were spending money on foreign technology to modernise production, and that in time the export of more attractive goods would rectify the trade balance. This assumption unfortunately proved unfounded.

■ As in all post-communist countries, if to a lesser extent, opinion in the Czech Republic took a turn to the left. In the parliamentary elections on the 31st May – 1st June 1996, ODS still emerged as the largest party (29,6% of the vote), but this time the Czech Social Democratic Party, led by Miloš Zeman, was close on its heels (26,4%). The parties of the governing coalition won a total of only 99 mandates as against 101 opposition mandates divided between the Social Democrats, the Communists and the Republicans. With substantial assistance from President Václav Havel, the democratic parliamentary parties reached an agreement by which the Social Democrats agreed to "tolerate" a minority right-wing government. In return, they obtained important positions in audit bodies and parliamentary committees, and their leader, Zeman, was elected chairman of the lower house.

The rise of the Social Democrats

■ Klaus's new government was in a very weak position. In parliament it only managed to push its bills through thanks to the vote of a single "disobedient" Social Democrat. Above all, however, it could not ignore growing economic problems that threatened the stability of the state budget. It attempted to control them by the restrictive measures contained in two "packages" (16th of April and 28th of May 1997), which cut wages in the state and state-funded sector, as well as welfare benefits, investment expenses etc.

Pitfalls of the "Czech way" of transforming the economy

■ These measures were very unpopular and caused great frustration. The government had assured the population that the transformation was already successful and complete, but was now telling people that the problems were only just beginning. There were naturally attempts to look back and analyse what had gone wrong. The main cause was identified as lying in the chosen form of privatisation, which in many cases had not provided firms with responsible owners or with capital, since the new owners had used up most of their funds for the purchase itself (if they had not simply used loans for the purchase, subsequently paid back from the assets of the firm itself). Unlike businessmen who have built up their firms from the beginning and are committed to them, those who acquired their property in the privatisation campaign often behaved in inexperienced or irresponsible ways, and proved unexpectedly incapable of controlling management. They were either not up to the job, or directly abused their position by the practice known as "tunnelling", i.e. siphoning off the firm's economic potential to the benefit of other companies. To minimise conflict while proceeding with such activities, they also put up no opposition to wage demands from employees. Work productivity did not increase. It also became clear that while Czech privatisation had been very rapid, it had not been thorough-going. Since Czech firms had already been suffering from major shortages of capital and obtained none from the new owners, unless these were foreign companies, they needed large loans. They thus became dependent on banks that were to a large extent owned by the state. The banks behaved with no greater caution or rationality than the businesses. Their managements knew that if they had trouble with bad loans, the state would step in to help them, and this is indeed what happened. The state paid out billions of crowns to save the banking sector, although several banks still collapsed as a result of the inexperience or fraudulent practices of their employees. Finally, the legal system proved insufficiently effective, and was unable to react quickly or efficiently enough to increasingly widespread abuses.

Criticism of the Klaus government

■ There is no doubt that many of these problems could have been tackled in the mid -90s, but a certain exhaustion after the stormy events of the preceding years (and especially the difficult process of dividing the state after the division of Czechoslovakia), together with an unjustified sense of complacency, seems to have prevented vigorous action. Disputes within the governing coalition also had a negative effect. The chairman of the KDU, Josef Lux, who became one of the most conspicuous figures on the political scene at the time, was particularly critical of what he considered the excessively liberal attitudes of Václav Klaus and ODS and their style of political behaviour. Nor was stability enhanced by frequent changes of ministers and incipient disputes within ODS itself. The government's feebleness was underlined by its confused reaction to a railwaymen's strike in the Spring of

The CR is accepted in NATO at a formal ceremony in the twon of Independence (the picture shows the defence ministers of the USA, ČR, Poland and Hungary - M. Albright, J. Kavan, J. Martony and B. Geremek)

1997, and the disillusion of the public was evident at a major protest demonstration against government policies called by the Bohemlan-Moravian Chamber of Trade Unions.

■ It was, however, internal party conflict that brought about the fall of the Klaus government. On the 27th of November 1997, reports were published alleging frauds in ODS party finances, including fictive sponsors and a secret bank account in Switzerland. The KDU left the coalition, and was soon followed by ODA (although ODA itself, always a small party, was soon hit by a similar scandal that led to its virtual disintegration). A split opened up in ODS, and on the 17th of January Klaus's party opponents met in Litomyšl to create a new party known as the Union of Freedom (US), and led by the former minister of the interior Jan Ruml. Klaus had already submitted his resignation on the 30th of November 1997, and it was the president who became the guarantee of continuity and stability, and once again contributed to finding a solution to the situation.

■ A new interim government, independent of political parties and headed by Josef Tošovský, up to that time governor of the Czech National Bank, was formed in December 1997.

M. Zeman's Social Democratic government

Both the main political forces undertook to respect it, so long as new elections were held as soon as possible. These took place on the 19th – 20th June 1998, resulting in victory for the ČSSD (32% of the vote), followed by ODS (28%), the KSČM (11%), the KDU (9%) and US (8,6%). The extremist republicans did not attract enough votes to gain a seat in the parliament, and ODA, too, found itself without a seat. Otherwise the situation in fact resembled that of two years before, since no political party proved able to find partners to create a majority government (despite that fact that theoretically a majority right-wing government could have been put together from ODS, US and the KDU, or a left-centre government from the ČSSD, KDU and US). Instead, the ČSSD made what was christened the "opposition agreement" with ODS, by which ODS guaranteed a certain tolerance towards a Social Democratic minority government. In exchange ODS obtained the chairmanship of the lower house, this time for Václav Klaus, and considerable influence on government decision-making. It also gained a promise that the ČSSD would draw up a reform of the electoral law to benefit the large parties, which would then have a better chance of creating majority governments.

Efforts to stabilise the political scene

■ The agreement between the ČSSD and ODS has often been criticised as a step that blurs the distinction between the governing and opposition elements of parliamentary democracy. Its supporters, however, have claimed that there was no alternative. In any event, its existence has led to the emergence of new civic initiatives to raise public consciousness.

Economic policies of the Zeman government

■ The first challenge facing Zeman's government was how to halt a significant economic decline. It has also had to cope with what was previously a relatively unknown phenomenon in the Czech Republic – unemployment, which has increased rapidly especially in some regions of Northern Bohemia and Moravia that were earlier dominated by coal-mining and heavy industry. It has tried to revive economic growth by the policy known as "revitalisation" of important concerns which have found themselves in deep difficulties but nonetheless have good production programmes and orders, and are of crucial importance for the development of employment in their regions. A Revitalisation Agency has been established to draw up special programmes that include negotiating solutions with creditors, and finding funds to allow fulfilment of existing orders and restructuring . This programme has not, however, produced any successes yet. Nor have there been any convincing results from the Clean Hands campaign, aimed at economic crime.

■ Zeman's cabinet has enjoyed greater success in attracting foreign investors to the country, and has also vigorously stepped up bank privatisation. The key issue will be how far the Czech economy will cope with the expected structural changes, and whether it will be able to compensate for the contraction of traditional sectors such as coal-mining and heavy industry by the expansion of sectors linked to the new information technologies. Certain positive signs are already discernible. Data for 1999 show that there was a slight growth in gross national product. Nevertheless, if the Czech Republic is to catch up with West European countries, it needs to increase the pace of its economic growth significantly (at a rate of 5% growth in GDP every year for 15–20 years). To help achieve such economic growth it will be necessary to complete privatisation, secure investments for key sectors of the national economy, speed up the building of infrastructure (especially connections to the main road and rail arteries in the EU) and develop information technologies. Reform of the pension system and the legal system are subjects of intensive debate. Above all there is general agreement that Czech society must became an "education society", that the number of university educated professionals must be increased, and that measures be taken to ensure that the Czech education system, highly effective at transferring knowledge, should also encourage creative thought and the ability to communicate.

■ On the 12th of March 1999, Czech foreign policy achieved one of its chief goals. Together with Hungary and Poland, the Czech Republic was accepted into NATO. It was soon apparent that this was no mere formality, since on the 24th of March the air-forces of the alliance launched their operation in Kosovo. Although the reactions of the Czech public were mixed, as a result of traditional pro-Serb sympathies going back to the 19th Century, the Czech Republic fulfilled its obligations to the alliance without exception. In December 1997, the Czech Republic received its official invitation to join the EU, and preliminary negotiations were initiated in March of the following year. At the beginning certain doubts were expressed as to whether the republic was moving fast enough in its adjustments to EU norms and laws. Now, however, it seems that delays have been overcome, and introduction of European legislation is going ahead at an ever accelerating tempo. There are therefore good grounds for believing that the Czech Republic will be ready for accession to the European Union in the year 2005, the date now considered the most likely for EU entry.

Prospects for the Czech economy

The ČR, NATO and the EU

■

PETR ČORNEJ

■

JIŘÍ POKORNÝ

■

A BRIEF
HISTORY
OF THE CZECH
LANDS
TO 2000

Translation from the Czech original by Anna Bryson
Jacket design and graphic design by Pravoslav Nesrovnal
Type-setting by Vladimír Vyskočil – KORŠACH
Printed by Ekon Jihlava
Published by the Práh Press, PO Box 46, 181 00 Prague 8,
as its 130th publication